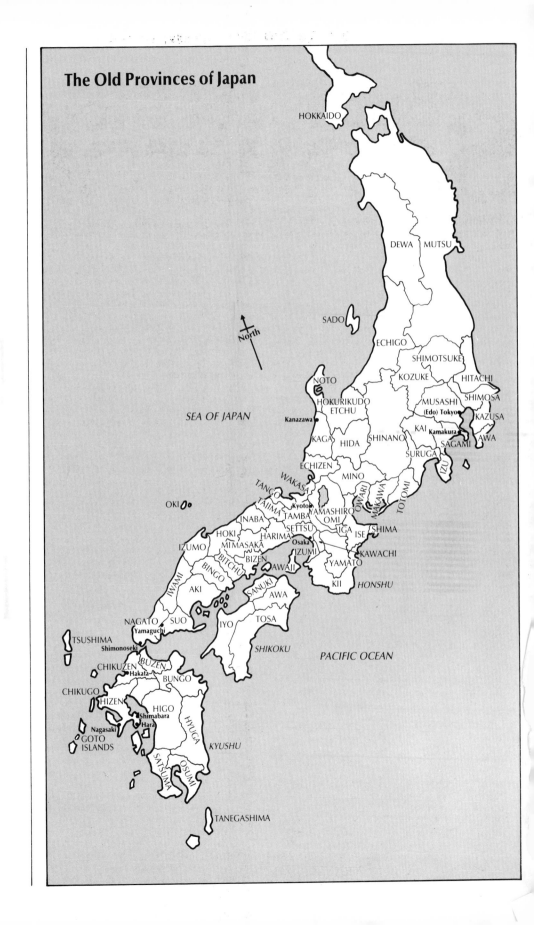

The Old Provinces of Japan

Battles of the Samurai

Battles of the
Samurai

Stephen Turnbull

ARMS AND ARMOUR PRESS
London New York Sydney

Dedicated to my son, Richard Turnbull

First published in Great Britain
in 1987 by Arms and Armour Press, Artillery House,
Artillery Row, London SW1P 1RT.

Distributed in the USA by Sterling Publishing Co. Inc.,
2 Park Avenue, New York, NY 10016.

Distributed in Australia by
Capricorn Link (Australia) Pty. Ltd., P.O. Box 665,
Lane Cove, New South Wales 2066, Australia.

British Library Cataloguing in Publication Data:
Turnbull, S. R.
Battles of the samurai
1. Samurai—History
2. Japan—History—Tokugawa period, 1600–1868
I. Title
952'.025   DS871.78
ISBN 0-85368-826-5

Jacket illustration: a scene from a a hanging scroll
depicting the exploits of Sengoku Hidehisa (1551–1614)
during the Shikoku campaign of 1581. (Ueda Castle
Historical Museum, Ueda, Nagano Prefecture; photograph
by the author.)

The illustrations in this book have been collected
from many sources, and vary in quality owing to the variety
of circumstances under which they were taken and preserved.
As a result, certain of the illustrations are not of the
standard to be expected from the best of today's equipment,
materials and techniques. They are nevertheless included
for their inherent information value, to provide an
authentic visual coverage of the subject.

Edited and designed by DAG Publications Ltd.
Designed by David Gibbons; layout by Anthony A. Evans;
edited by Michael Boxall; typeset by Typesetters
(Birmingham) Ltd., camerawork by E&M Graphics, North
Fambridge, Essex; printed and bound in Great Britain by
R. J. Acford Ltd., Chichester.

Contents

List of Maps

Introduction

The samurai of Japan were men of war. Whatever other roles they may have adopted throughout their history – administrator, patron of the arts, landowner or politician, the waging of war was the skill by which they were judged, and the means by which they ensured their own personal survival.

In this study of samurai battles I have chosen to concentrate on the sixteenth century, the *Sengoku-jidai*, or 'Age of the Country at War', but have, of necessity, preceded this discussion with two battles from the earlier period which illustrate the developing tradition under which the later battles were conducted. My choice of battles therefore shows the developments in tactics, strategy and weapons that made their mark on Japanese history between 1180 and 1600.

Throughout this time Japan was ruled, as it had been since the dawn of written history, by a remote and god-like emperor, whose governing function was supplanted in the year 1192 by a succession of dynasties of shoguns, the well-known term for the military dictator. The first shogun, Minamoto Yoritomo, took power as the result of a fierce civil war, but in the four centuries that followed, the shogunal families (all of whom claimed descent from the Minamoto) and the notion of the shogunate itself, underwent many changes. By the early sixteenth century the weakness of the Ashikaga shogunate was such that samurai landlords, called *daimyo*, were able to rule their own territories as if they were independent princes, and make war on their neighbours.

From these men came a considerable number of innovations in warfare, brought about by desperate need. Life was a succession of wars, involving raids on neighbours, the taking of castles and the giving of battle. These battles of the sixteenth century were the testbeds for new ideas, fought against the gorgeous backdrop of samurai history and tradition.

This book examines nine major battles and several minor conflicts. At Kurikara we see a classic, formal battle, conducted exactly according to precedent and tradition, but with an unexpected sting in the tail. The fall of Kamakura shows us noble deeds mixed with self-interest on a grand and tragic scale. We leap into the sixteenth century with Okehazama, to introduce the genius of Oda Nobunaga. The following chapter, which describes for the first time in English the Fourth Battle of Kawanaka-jima, shows us a colossal example of the mighty Takeda war-machine in action, of which Mikata-ga-Hara, which follows, is a neater illustration. Anegawa shows us another 'modern' battle, with firearms and troop movements on a large scale, but made more personal with the gallant Makara family. The famous Battle of Nagashino writes a new chapter in Japanese military history, which we conclude with the tragic end of Takeda Katsuyori. The relief of Shizugatake and the the great strategy needed for its achievement bespeak Hideyoshi's talents, and we end with the great Battle of Sekigahara, and the desperate chess-game of seizing castles that almost prevented it from taking place.

The names of many of the battles will be familiar to the reader from the author's previous work, but for the first time he will have the opportunity to study these important conflicts using almost exclusively Japanese sources; these have enabled the author to present to an English-speaking public the first ever full accounts of such engagements as the Fourth Battle of Kawanakajima, Kurikara and Mikata-ga-Hara.

At the end of each chapter I have included directions for visiting each of the sites I have described, should any reader be fortunate enough to follow in my footsteps.

There are many people to thank for enabling me to bring this about. The staff of the Department of Oriental Manuscripts and Printed Books at the British Library have been particularly helpful in the supply of source material. Much more has come from Japan, through the army of friends and contacts I made while doing fieldwork in Japan. This book could not have been written without the first-hand experience of the sites which I was able to gain in the spring of 1986, and such a busy schedule could not have been entertained without the support and co-operation of many individuals and organizations.

First, thanks must go to Mrs Nahoko Kitajima, whose arrangements made my visit efficient and effective; to Yukito Kaiki and Nobuyo Ichifuji who took me to Kurikara; to Mr Kazukata Ogino, who showed me Nagashino and supplied aerial photographs; to Mr Kitahara who took me to Anegawa and Shizugatake; to Dr Myra Shackley of Leicester University, for allowing me to use the fruits of her researches into the evidence of battle damage from the Zaimokusa site; to the staff of the Sekigahara Public Museum, who helped me plan my route round the battlefield, and to the dozens of anonymous taxi-drivers, bus-drivers, site guides and members of the public who understood my appalling Japanese and pointed me in the right direction at the appropriate moment!

Above all I wish to thank my dear wife, Jo and my children, Alex, Richard and Katy, whose love and support makes everything worthwhile and who provide the happy home to which the traveller returns.

Right: Attacking through mud. This illustration from the *Ehon Taiko-ki* shows samurai, whose swastika *mon* (badge) identifies them as follows of Wakizaka Yasuharu (1554–1626), wearing a form of snow-shoes to give them a better grip on muddy ground.

8

1183

The Battle of Kurikara

The Battle of Kurikara was fought on 2 June 1183 on the slopes of a mountain called Tonamiyama, by which name the battle is also known. It was probably the largest battle fought on Japanese soil up to that time, and marked a decisive turning-point in the great civil war known as the Gempei War. It is also a unique example of a stylized formal battle, though this is not without a subtle purpose!

The Gempei War

The Gempei War, which was fought from 1180 until 1185, takes its name from the two clans who were opposed. On one side were the Minamoto, and on the other, the Taira. 'Minamoto-clan' and 'Taira-clan' are respectively *Genji* and *Heike*, in the Chinese readings of the characters used for their names, so combining the elements we obtain the compound Gempei, which is also used for that particular period of Japanese history. The Gempei War may remind readers of England's Wars of the Roses, an analogy that is strengthened by the Taira use of red for their flags and the Minamoto's use of white.

In the centuries preceding the Gempei War Japan was ruled, as it had been since time immemorial, by the sacred person of the emperor, but from about AD 1100, although power was still nominally in the hands of the emperor, the decisions of government had been made by a complex bureaucracy of courtiers, nearly all of whom belonged to the Fujiwara family. Court politics were often made more confusing by the presence of one or even more ex-emperors, because it had become the accepted practice for the emperor to abdicate while he was still young. This freed a vigorous young man from the constant round of ceremonial and religious ritual which, as a living god, the emperor was required to perform. This practice meant of course that succession rarely passed directly from father to son, and the presence of numerous heirs to the throne, supplied by imperial concubines, kept up a ready supply of 'Young Pretenders', should any rebel against the incumbent emperor wish to try his luck with his own 'legitimate emperor'. The rules of the game were simple: the faction that controlled the emperor were noble loyalists. Whoever opposed him were rebels, who must be destroyed. The secret of success was to choose your emperor wisely.

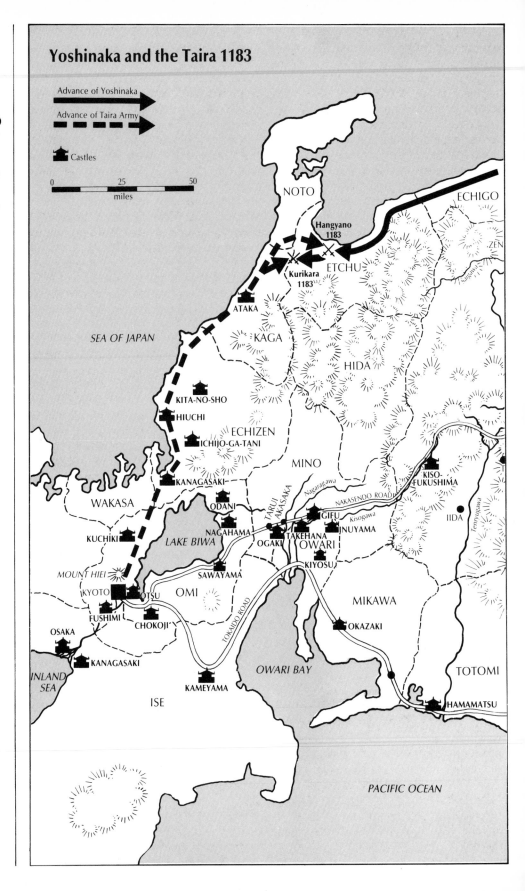

1183
THE BATTLE OF KURIKARA

Yoshinaka and the Taira 1183

Advance of Yoshinaka

Advance of Taira Army

Castles

0   25   50
miles

NOTO

ECHIGO

Hangyano
1183

ETCHU

Kurikara
1183

ATAKA

SEA OF JAPAN

KAGA

HIDA

KITA-NO-SHO

HIUCHI

ECHIZEN

ICHIJO-GA-TANI

MINO

KISO-
FUKUSHIMA

KANAGASAKI

IIDA

WAKASA

ODANI

NAGAHAMA

TARUI
AKASAKA

Nagaragawa

NAKASENDO ROAD

GIFU

Kisogawa

INUYAMA

Tenryugawa

KUCHIKI

LAKE BIWA

OGAKI

TAKEHANA

OWARI

SAWAYAMA

KIYOSU

MOUNT HIEI

KYOTO

OTSU

OMI

MIKAWA

FUSHIMI

CHOKOJI

OKAZAKI

OSAKA

KANAGASAKI

TOKAIDO ROAD

OWARI BAY

TOTOMI

INLAND
SEA

KAMEYAMA

HAMAMATSU

ISE

PACIFIC OCEAN

Several of these rebellions during the eleventh century were put down by members of the Taira clan. The family was of imperial descent, and had recently begun to imitate the Fujiwara by marrying its daughters to imperial princes. It also continued to serve the court well in military terms, helping to put down revolts and riots by the armies of warrior monks from the old monasteries of Kyoto and Nara, who would assault the capital when they had a grievance against the emperor or against one another. By 1150 the clan leader, Taira Kiyomori, enjoyed a central position in the imperial Court, and was effectively the ruler of Japan. Furthermore, his daughter was soon to make him an Imperial Grandfather.

Historically the Taira had tended to settle in the west of Japan. They were accomplished sailors, and helped the trade with China by clearing pirates from the waters of the Inland Sea. Their rivals, the Minamoto, who were descended from a different imperial ancestor, were dominant in the East, where life was every bit as hard for a warrior, if not harder, because there were campaigns to conduct against rival clans and the aboriginal Ainu people.

All such clans, of whom the Taira and the Minamoto were most influential, maintained armies of hereditary retainers called 'samurai', 'those who serve', which is the origin of the word that has come to be used to describe any member of the Japanese warrior class. These samurai, who were well-trained mounted archers and swordsmen, were backed up by many more footsoldiers who were comparatively poorly equipped and were recruited from the farmers who tilled the samurai lord's ricefields. The samurai wore armour made from small iron scales tied together and lacquered, then combined into armour plates by binding them together with silk or leather cords. This classic 'samurai armour', which changed little over the centuries, provided a strong but light protection for the body.

In 1156 the Minamoto challenged the Taira's supremacy in Kyoto, and began a revolt against the Taira in the name of an imperial heir. It began well, but was soon crushed by the Taira samurai, who executed the ringleaders, and then attempted to exterminate all the members of the Minamoto family. In fact only a handful of Minamoto boys escaped to the East and safety. As these boys grew to manhood they dreamed of revenging their fathers and uncles, and in 1180 further outbreaks developed into a full-scale civil war. One of these, in Kyoto, ended with the Minamoto soundly defeated at the First Battle of Uji, but another rising in the East was more successful. It was led by the young and skilful Minamoto Yoritomo, who put to flight a huge Taira army sent to chastise him. The Minamoto launched a night attack on the Taira camp near the Fujigawa, the river that flows beside Mount Fuji, and were helped by a flock of waterfowl which flew over the Taira camp and alarmed them, so the small surprise raid became a rout.

Kiso Yoshinaka

Yoritomo had a cousin called Yoshinaka, who had escaped from the Taira not to the East but to Shinano province in the mountainous interior of Japan. Through Shinano, along the course of the old Nakasendo Road, flowed the River Kiso, and Yoshinaka adopted the surname Kiso instead of Minamoto. In 1180 he heard of the revolt by the Minamoto in Kyoto, and received a copy of the imperial proclamation by the Minamoto's 'Pretender' Prince Mochihito, asking all right-minded men to rise and chastise the Taira clan, thus lending legitimacy to the rebellion. Not wishing to be outdone by any of his relatives, Yoshinaka gathered an army from among his tough mountain-men, and began to attack and seize for himself any lands owned by the Taira family or their supporters in the provinces of Shinano and Echigo. He carefully avoided striking towards the southeast and the sphere of influence of his cousin Yoritomo. Instead, elated by success he turned to the west, and invaded Etchu, Kaga and Echizen, sweeping all before him, stopping only when scarcely sixty miles from Kyoto itself.

His advance had stagnated under an enemy that struck down friend and foe alike – famine. By the end of 1181 two years of fighting over the precious ricelands of Japan had taken their toll of the rice crop around the capital. The fields had been looted and burned by both sides, and the

1183
THE BATTLE OF KURIKARA

1183
THE BATTLE OF KURIKARA

Right: Kiso Yoshinaka. This fine equestrian statue of Minamoto 'Kiso' Yoshinaka stands in the grounds of the Hachiman Shrine near the battlefield. It shows the armour that would have been worn at the battle by a high-ranking samurai, and is authentic except for one detail – the sculptor has given him a *sashimono* banner on the back of his armour, which was not introduced until the sixteenth century. Yoshinaka visited this shrine before the battle and made an offering to Hachiman the war-god, who was the patron of the Minamoto clan.

farmers had been taken as soldiers for the armies. The Taira retreated to Kyoto, and Yoshinaka returned home to the more prosperous Shinano, leaving garrisons of troops at strategic points along the coast of the Sea of Japan. Minamoto Yoritomo, who was based in Kamakura, fared better, because these heartlands of the Minamoto family had not been ravaged, but there was no question of an attack on Kyoto. No army could live off the land in a starved country. So 1182 passed without war.

The March to Kurikara
As the effects of the famine subsided the Taira began to think about how they could punish Yoshinaka for his depredations. In 1181 the leader of the clan, Imperial Grand-father Taira Kiyomori, had died of a fever, his last words being, 'Place upon my tomb the head of Yoritomo,' but his successors looked far less capable than he had been of fulfilling his last request, or even of chastising Yoritomo's wild mountain cousin. His eldest son had predeceased him, so his second son became the new clan chief. Taira Munemori was so incompetent that it was rumoured that he was not a true Taira, but in fact the son of an umbrella merchant.

The expedition to the north against Yoshinaka was not to be led by the questionable Munemori, but by his son, Taira Koremori, whose previous experience of war cannot have given anyone grounds for great confidence in him. It was he who had led the army against Minamoto Yoritomo in

Left: A weapon from Kurikara. This rusty blade from either a *naginata* (glaive) or a very long sword was found on the site of the Battle of Kurikara. Here, it is held by a priest from the Fudo-ji, a Shingon temple on Tonamiyama, in the Kurikara Pass.

1180, and had been forced to flee from the waterfowl of the Fujigawa. The second in command was his uncle, Taira Michimori, who bore the title of Echizen-no-kami, or Feudal Lord of Echizen, the province which Yoshinaka had conquered, so it was no more than appropriate that he should play his part in the noble undertaking. With them were five other notable family members: Taira Tsunemasa, Kiyofusa, Tomonori, Tadanori and Tamemori.

They had under them a nucleus of well-trained samurai who had served the Emperor against the monks, and had fought in the early battles of the Gempei War, but famine and war had taken their toll, and there were not enough of them, so attempts were made to recruit or levy

troops for the unenviable task of the northern campaign. Estates were denuded of workers, bringing further risk of famine as men were drafted in from Taira lands hundreds of miles away. The grand total of this motley crew is supposed to have been 100,000, an impossible total which exceeds the most gigantic armies of the sixteenth century, but even if this figure were divided by ten it is difficult to gauge how many arrived, and how many existed only as names on a recruiting officer's list. Nevertheless the Taira high command seemed well satisfied, and set out with this army from Kyoto on 10 May 1183.

Yoshinaka, meanwhile, remained in Shinano. He had recently been joined by another Minamoto veteran, Yukiie, who

Right: Tomoe Gozen. Tomoe Gozen was the wife of Kiso Yoshinaka, and fought by his side in all his battles. She is an almost unique example of a female warrior in samurai history.

was his uncle. We can regard him as Yoshinaka's second in command, although he may not have proved to be a great asset to his nephew, as he had been defeated by the Taira in a battle in 1181. Another character who rode with Yoshinaka deserves mention. This was his wife, Tomoe Gozen, an almost unique example of a female samurai. She is recorded as having been both beautiful and brave, and as having fought by Yoshinaka's side in all his battles. Yoshinaka was also always accompanied by four faithful companions, known

as the *shitenno*. Their names were Imai Kanehira (his foster-brother), Higuchi Kanemitsu, Tate Chikatada and Nenoi Yukichika.

At the end of March 1183 Yoshinaka received news of an army marching to confront him. This was not the Taira, who were still recruiting their Grand Army in the West, but the army of his cousin, Yoritomo, who was notionally head of the clan, and who believed implicitly in the old Chinese proverb that there could not be two suns in heaven. Yoshinaka advanced to meet the

threat and, fortunately for the family, chose conciliation as his weapon. He sent a message to Yoritomo, whose troops had entered Shinano, in which he pointed out the obvious fact that if they were united the Minamoto could crush the Taira, while divided they would most likely fall. With two strong Minamoto armies between them ready to fall on Kyoto from two directions, a family feud was the last thing they needed. Yoritomo accepted the statement in good faith, and withdrew his troops under Yoshinaka's assurances of good intentions,

backed up by Yoshinaka sending his son to Kamakura as a hostage. Soon after this Yoshinaka heard that the Taira army was advancing along the coast from Kyoto.

Our main source for the campaign is the classic Japanese epic poem *Heike Monogatari*. *Heike Monogatari* is something of a Buddhist parable, relating the long story of the eventual destruction of the Taira family as a result of evil fate. It is very sympathetically written, and never more so as when it describes the first few days of the progress of the Taira's 'Grand Army'. They took the road up the west side of Lake Biwa, under Mount Hiei, a well-used route which is followed today by the train. The Taira army, which was deserting as rapidly as it was advancing, had been appallingly badly organized. No plans had been made for supplies of food, so foraging had to begin while they were only nine miles from Kyoto. The account in *Heike Monogatari* describes them as a horde of pillagers, devastating lands in provinces that were their own, Taira territory, whence they had press-ganged the farmers.

As they passed Lake Biwa the two commanders pressed on, but their subordinates took the opportunity of a little sightseeing and other aesthetic pursuits. The *Heike Monogatari* is not condemnatory in its tone, it is even approving as it describes (in Sadler's classic translation) the behaviour of Taira Tsunemasa who wished to 'calm his mind in the midst of these alarms and disorders'. He and his companions took a boat out to the island of Chikubushima, where he wrote poetry and sang. So exquisite was his performance that the goddess Myojin, to whom the place was dedicated, appeared beside him in the form of a white dragon. Tsunemasa was an accomplished poet, as were many of the Taira clan who were near to the imperial court by birth or duties, which gentles somewhat the traditional image of the fierce and bloodthirsty samurai warrior, but even so this was insensitive behaviour by one whose army was falling apart.

Meanwhile the advance guard of the Taira was reaching the border with Wakasa province, which was 2,500 feet up on the top of a high ridge. At this point today the railway goes through one of the world's longest tunnels. In 1183 the Taira soldiers

1183
THE BATTLE OF KURIKARA

would have had a last view of home from the summit, then descended the northern slopes which led to enemy territory. (See map on page 10.)

From here the Taira hugged the coast of the Sea of Japan. This was longer than an inland route, but safer. The first sign of the Minamoto was an outpost, a simple stockade fortress called Hiuchi, built on rocky crags, and well defended. The Minamoto had built a dam to create a moat, which hindered the Taira assault until a traitor fired an arrow telling them how to breach the dam and run off the water. Hiuchi fell on about 20 May, and some five days later the Taira troops entered Kaga province to meet another Minamoto army at Ataka. The Taira were again victorious and the Minamoto withdrew, but were undismayed, for, like Hiuchi, the skirmish provided Yoshinaka with just the information he needed. He now knew the strength and the direction of advance of the Taira army. Their route was bypassing the mountainous interior (now the Haku-san National Park), to turn east across the narrow neck of the Noto peninsula and on to Yoshinaka's territory of Etchu province. It was also more than likely that they intended to cross the mountain range by the Pass of Kurikara.

The Battle of Kurikara

The general area around Kurikara is still the main line of communication across the mountains of this part of Japan. From the triple peaks of Haku-san, thirty miles to the south, the rugged mountains gradually decline to forested hills. The main railway line today bears east after leaving Kanazawa and passes through the ridge by means of a tunnel to Tonami. Kurikara station is just west of the tunnel. The pass of Kurikara, which is now a modern road, is somewhat to the south of the line:

At this point we have to examine closely our sources for the battle. Spohr (1967) working probably from the chronicle *Gempei Seisuki* has the Taira army approach the Kurikara Pass from the east, following a victory over the Minamoto at Hangyano. (This is the interpretation the present author made in *The Samurai – A Military History*). The *Heike Monogatari* has them approaching from the west, which is far more likely. The confusion probably

arises from the fact that before approaching Kurikara the Taira army was divided into two. The larger part, under Koremori, crossed the Kurikara Pass and fought the battle. The smaller contingent entered Etchu through Noto province further to the north, and did in fact gain a minor victory which was totally nullified by the defeat at Kurikara. This interpretation is supported by the pamphlet about the battle published by the Fudo-ji temple at Tonamiyama's summit, on which the author has based the map on page 16. It is also strongly supported by common sense when one visits the site. Yoshinaka wanted to stop the Taira advance, not slow down a retreat.

Yoshinaka's army advanced to Kurikara from the east, and observed that the Taira were approaching the summit of Tonamiyama up the Pass of Kurikara. Yoshinaka had a plan, and for it to work the Taira had to remain on the top of Kurikara Pass until nightfall. So he erected thirty white banners on Kurosaka hill, about a mile away, to make the Taira think they would be faced with a vastly superior force when they descended. The Taira commanders drew the conclusion he intended, and decided to rest on the safety of the mountain and water their horses.

While making his preparations near Kurosaka, Yoshinaka observed a Shinto shrine among the trees, which turned out to be dedicated to Hachiman, the god of war, who was the patron of the Minamoto clan. This was a very good omen, so Yoshinaka visited the shrine (which still exists) and paid his respects to the deity. As if in response three wild doves fluttered out

The Battle of Kurikara

卍 Traditional sign for a Buddhist Temple

鳥 Shin'to Shrine

Tonamiyama
Fudo-ji
Kurosaka Hill
Pass of Kurikara
Kurikara Valley

Retreat of Taira Army

Yoshinaka's Advance

■ Yoshinaka
◪ Taira

0   Mile   1

Left: From Tonamiyama to Kurosaka. Looking east from the summit of Tonamiyama to the hill of Kurosaka, where Yoshinaka erected banners to discourage the Taira from descending. Kurosaka is the hill just to the left of the ground where the trees have been cleared, probably for a road. The 'formal' battle was fought in the foreground of this picture, which is now all woodland.

from the trees. Doves are regarded as the messengers of the god of war (in strange contrast to the Western notion of doves of peace) so this was doubly encouraging.

Returning from Kurosaka Yoshinaka divided his forces. One detachment was sent on a wide sweep to approach the Taira from the rear. Three units were detached to conceal themselves at the foot of Kurikara valley, which lay beneath the pass. The rest he held centrally. But how was Yoshinaka to cover all these movements and hold the Taira in position? His solution was both daring and amusing. He would conceal his manoeuvres by fighting a battle! He would give battle to the Taira in a manner so formal, so stylized and so traditional, that there would be no risk of his side being defeated, nor any opportunity for the Taira to realize that the whole purpose was to confine them to this small area until night fell. Yoshinaka knew his history, and the demands of samurai tradition. The battle would begin with a duel of arrows, followed by individual combat. The proud Taira would give it their full concentration, hoping thereby to earn for themselves a name in the epic poetry that would be written about them in the future.

So the two armies faced each other in full battle array, at a distance of about 350 yards, but neither side advanced. After a time, fifteen picked samurai from the Minamoto came forward between the armies, and each fired a signalling arrow at the Taira lines. Signalling arrows had a large wooden head, perforated with holes, which whistled as they flew through the air. At this, fifteen men of the Taira responded similarly. Then thirty Minamoto samurai advanced and fired arrows, against whom the Taira sent thirty more, and so on, fifty to a hundred. Then these hundred engaged one another in combat. It was all very splendid, and an excellent way of wasting time. The Taira joined in enthusiastically. Their well-educated, aristocratic samurai would have been brought up on the old epics about their ancestors, of how they fought brave combats and took noble heads, and now this rough mountain-man was allowing them to exercise their military skills in the most correct manner!

Throughout the day of 2 June 1183 there continued challenges to combat and any amount of brave deeds, all the stuff of legend, fought just below the slope of the hill, which the Minamoto dared not permit

1183
THE BATTLE OF KURIKARA

Right: Beware of the bull! Having ensured that the Taira stayed on top of Tonamiyama, Yoshinaka stampeded a herd of oxen along Kurikara Pass towards them. The animals were enraged by having lighted torches tied to their horns. These dummy oxen stand today on the site of the battle.

Right: Yoshinaka's surprise attack. This painting, at the Fudo-ji on Kurikara Pass, shows the effect of Yoshinaka's 'fiery bulls' on the Taira samurai.

them to leave. Not that the Taira had anything to fear. To the south of their position the ground fell away over rocky crags into a deep valley, from which it would be impossible for the Minamoto to launch an attack. They were right. Yoshinaka had no intention of attacking up the Kurikara valley. He meant to force them down into this death-trap, making the narrow paths into it the only way the Taira could go.

In early summer in Japan night falls at about 6 p.m., and there is effectively no twilight. As the sun set Yoshinaka's encircling force arrived at the rear, well supplied with many more banners than would normally be carried by a small mobile force. As the Taira reacted to this surprise they met a further shock in front. Yoshinaka had heard of his cousin's success with the waterfowl of the Fujigawa. He now tried the same trick, but with a much stronger stimulus!

His men had rounded up a herd of oxen and tied torches to their horns. The torches were fired, and the enraged oxen whipped off along the pass. (The *Heike Monogatari*, strangely enough, omits any description of this colourful incident.) Some Taira samurai were knocked clean off the path by the frantic herd. Meanwhile the soldiers on the northern slope, who had been such gentlemen until then, charged forward in a screaming rush. There was nowhere for the Taira samurai to go except down into the valley of Kurikara, which they thought had a safe exit. But the paths petered out, and Yoshinaka's detached forces were waiting for them in the dark. Thousands were killed in the confusion, and one senior Taira commander met his death when Higuchi Kanemisu killed Taira Tamemori in the pursuit. In the words of *Heike Monogatari*: 'As those behind could not see those in front,

they thought there must be a road at the bottom of the valley, and so the whole army went down one after another, son after father, brother after brother and retainer after lord, horses and men falling on top of one another and piling up in heaps upon heaps.'

So Kiso Yoshinaka defeated a Taira army, and its remnants, together with the other, smaller, part of their original force, eventually managed to get back to Kyoto, but not until Yoshinaka had inflicted further defeats upon them. Shortly afterwards Yoshinaka entered Kyoto in triumph, the first member of the Minamoto family to do so. Kurikara was the watershed of the Gempei War, and a foretaste of what was to come.

Right: Kurikara Valley. To the south of Tonamiyama the ground drops away steeply into the Kurikara valley. Yoshinaka drove the Taira down into this valley, from which few escaped.

Kurikara today

Kurikara is best approached by car, from either Toyama or Kanazawa. The pass of Kurikara winds up over Tonamiyama as it did in 1183. You may stop and visit the Fudo-ji temple, where there are items connected with the battle. A little further on you come to the summit. The site of the Taira camp is marked with a monument. There are good views as far as the sea and, on payment of 100 yen, a loudspeaker gives a raucous commentary on the battle. There are also life-size replicas of the famous bulls! The Hachiman Shrine is a short drive away. It is an interesting building, quite unpretentious, and has a very fine bronze statue of Kiso Yoshinaka.

1333

The Battle of Kamakura

The second battle I have chosen to discuss is the Battle of Kamakura in 1333. Kamakura was mentioned in the previous chapter as being the headquarters of Yoshinaka's cousin, Minamoto Yoritomo, and this gives the first clue as to why a desperate struggle for the capture of the city should have taken place more than a century and a half later.

The End of the Gempei War

Minamoto Yoritomo was the ultimate victor in the Gempei War. He used his family members to defeat the Taira, and then turned against his relatives to seize absolute power for himself. Yoshinaka's victory at Kurikara is the perfect example of Yoritomo's strategy. Yoshinaka followed up his defeat of the Taira army by marching on Kyoto, and then caused such havoc in the capital that the ex-emperor was forced to call upon Minamoto Yoritomo to intervene, as Yoritomo was the only one who could withstand him. Yoritomo sent his brothers, Yoshitsune and Noriyori, against Yoshinaka, whom they defeat and killed at the Second Battle of Uji in 1184.

From the destruction of his cousin, Yoritomo turned rapidly to the destruction of the Taira, which was finally accomplished at the sea battle of Dan-no-Ura in 1185. Yoritomo then assumed the title of shogun, 'commander-in-chief', an ancient rank bestowed temporarily on generals who went off to vanquish rebels on behalf of the emperor. Yoritomo made this temporary commission a permanent one, hereditary in his family. It was designed to eclipse the secular authority of the emperor and his imperial court, and place the samurai class firmly in control of Japan's destiny without recourse to the political marriages and court intrigue which the Taira had adopted from the Fujiwara as their style of government. The institution of the Shogunate, or *bakufu*, lasted until the mid nineteenth century, although with many vicissitudes and several gaps, but only one dynasty. All claimants to the position of shogun had to be descended from the Minamoto, which could be demonstrated by the three ruling houses that achieved shogunal status: the Minamoto themselves, the Ashikaga, and the Tokugawa. When there was no legitimacy of descent the current ruler had to act as shogunal regent, and it is one such occasion, the regency, or *shikken*, of the Hojo family, that provides the background to the Battle of Kamakura.

Kamakura

Minamoto Yoritomo died in 1192 following a riding accident. His death came as a great shock to the Minamoto, and effectively dealt a death-blow to them as a ruling house; they managed to provide only two more shoguns, both of whom were firmly under the control of the Hojo, the family of Yoritomo's widow. The Hojo were to supply ten regents between 1199 and 1333.

Like Yoritomo, their capital was Kamakura which lies on the coast of Sagami Bay, separated from today's Tokyo Bay by a short peninsula. From the twelfth to the fourteenth centuries the important fact about Kamakura's position was that it was a good three hundred miles from Kyoto, the imperial capital. This gave Yoritomo's administration, and the Hojo *shikken*, complete independence in how they ran the country. Kyoto was relegated to the status of the emperor's home. All the important decisions were made in Kamakura, set in the heartlands of the fierce Eastern Warriors. In fact the century and a half between 1192 and 1333 is known as the 'Kamakura Period' of Japanese history.

In its heyday, as the administrative capital of Japan, Kamakura grew rapidly and numerous important edifices, which today make Kamakura one of the most fascinating Japanese cities to visit, date from the Kamakura Period. As the Battle was fought within the city itself, it is worth examining its general layout, and noting which of the

1333
THE BATTLE OF KAMAKURA

Right: The Great Buddha of Kamakura. The fighting in the Battle of Kamakura was carried on around this famous statue, which in 1333 was enclosed within a wooden temple hall. A succession of storms and *tsunami* waves removed the temple during the following century, leaving the Buddha as it is today.

prominent tourist sites of today witnessed the fighting in 1333.

The town is squeezed in by mountains on three sides and the sea on a fourth. The high ground around Kamakura is nowhere very high, but is everywhere composed of very steep, conical forested hills that seem to rise suddenly from flat land, and from the air look like beached whales. Kamakura is surrounded by a cluster of such hills crammed together, one on top of another. This interesting topography is best appreciated from the train, which winds its way through tunnels and cuttings to reach the city, and these hills were no less important in 1333, as they formed the main, natural outer defences of the *bakufu* headquarters.

Through these hills in 1333 were seven passes, the *nana-kiridoshi*, guarded by checkpoints. Starting at the south-western corner a large promontory called Inamuragasaki protrudes into the sea. There is a road through Inamuragasaki nowadays, but in 1333 the only approach from the southwest was a pass just to the north called the Gokuraku-ji Pass, after the temple of Gokuraku-ji which lies at its mouth. One of Gokuraku-ji's abbots, Nonsho, who died in 1303, was renowned for his public works, including the cutting, or more probably

enlarging, of the Gokuraku-ji Pass. The pass dwindles to a footpath as one reaches the top, and could obviously be defended with relative ease.

The western approach to Kamakura was covered by the Daibutsu Pass, which drops down beside one of Kamakura's most famous sights, the Great Buddha. This huge and beautiful bronze statue witnessed the fighting in 1333, although none of the combatants would have seen it as one does today. At that time it was concealed within a wooden temple building, much like the other Great Buddha at the Todai-ji in Nara. Two years after the Battle, in 1335, and again in 1368, violent storms all but wrecked the building, and then in 1495 a *tsunami*, the so-called 'tidal wave', swept away all remnants of the structure to leave the Buddha sitting in the open air.

The northern entrances to Kamakura, which were the most important, were made through the Kewaizaka Pass, the Kamegayatsuka Pass and the Kobukorozaka Pass. These are important routes nowadays for road and rail. The Asahina Pass to the northeast is supposed by legend to have been dug in one night by the herculean Asahina Yoshihide, sone of the 'female samurai' Tomoe Gozen, mentioned in the previous

Left: Gokuraku-ji Pass. The Gokuraku-ji Pass, which covered the entrance to Kamakura from the west, was one of the most stubbornly defended of the Seven Passes. The successful resistance conducted here led to Nitta Yoshisada's 'miraculous' flank attack round Inamuragaski. This view is taken from the highest point, looking back down the pass towards the sea.

23

一
二

1333
THE BATTLE OF KAMAKURA

Right: Kamakura. The whole of the area shown in this view of Kamakura became the battlefield once the Imperialist troops broke into the city. On the far right is the cape of Inamuragasaki, site of Nitta Yoshisada's offering to the Sun-Goddess, and his subsequent advance.

chapter in connection with Yoshinaka. It is more likely to have been cut in about 1241, under the direction of the Hojo Regents. The last pass, the Nagoe, to the east, is now obscured by the railway which heads off down the peninsula.

In 1333 the town of Kamakura was centred around a long avenue, called Wakamiya-Oji, leading down to the sea from the Tsurugaoka Hachiman Shrine. Hachiman, as noted in our discussion of Yoshinaka, was the patron deity of the Minamoto, so it is not surprising that Yoritomo richly endowed this foundation, and was also instrumental in having the avenue built so that his infant son could be carried in state for his dedication ceremony. The shrine is also associated with the tragic fall of the Minamoto, when Yoritomo's second son was assassinated there in 1219. The shrine, and Wakamiya Avenue, are still the centre of Kamakura.

The Kemmu Restoration

Dynasties of shoguns, or regents for that matter, were not always challenged exclusively by other samurai families. On occasions the current emperor attempted to make the imperial dream come true, whereby the rule of the shogun would be ended and the emperor would rule as in olden days. An early attempt in 1221 by the ex-emperor, Go-Toba, was crushed in remarkably short time by the *bakufu* samurai, whose leaders sent an army against Kyoto, and defeated the imperialists at the Third Battle of Uji and other minor struggles.

A century later the ruling emperor, Go-Daigo, tried again, and this time the *bakufu*'s reaction was less decisive. Much had happened to Japan, and to the Hojo *shikken*, in the century that had passed. They had had to face foreign invasion from the armada of the Mongol Emperor, Kublai Khan, which had been repulsed by a com-

bination of samurai bravery and divine intervention from the *kami-kaze*, the 'holy wind' which destroyed the Mongol fleet in a typhoon. Nor were the Hojo regents what they had been. The current regent was Hojo Takatoki (1303–33) who had assumed the *shikken* at the age of eight. A man of poor intelligence and weak morals, his reputation no doubt encouraged Go-Daigo to try his hand, and Go-Daigo's raising of the flag of revolt against their decadent regency found many supporters. Obviously there would have been a good deal of self-interest on their part, for to have been seen to help a grateful emperor against an unpopular regency that was doomed anyway was likely to bring reward and privilege.

The arms and armour of the samurai had not changed much since the Gempei War, nor had the samurai notions of honour and tradition. The greatest samurai principle was loyalty to one's master, and one

samurai who supported Go-Daigo when the revolt began, and continued to be loyal even when things were going against the emperor's cause, was Kusunoki Masashige. Masashige held out against *bakufu* troops from a succession of mountain fortresses, and kept up his resistance in spite of Go-Daigo's being captured by the *bakufu* and a rival emperor being enthroned in his stead. This happened in 1332. Go-Daigo was exiled to the island of Oki, and the Kemmu Restoration, as it was called, looked as though it were over.

All would indeed have been lost had not Kusunoki Masashige continued his resistance in the form of a guerrilla campaign among the mountains of Yoshino. In 1333 three armies left Kamakura to destroy his latest hideouts, and defeated Kusunoki's comrade-in-arms, Prince Morinaga, Go-Daigo's son. But Kusunoki Masashige withdrew to a fortress called Chihaya, deep in

一
二

1333
THE BATTLE OF KAMAKURA

1333
THE BATTLE OF KAMAKURA

the mountains and forests of Kawachi province. Chihaya held out against every attempt to take it, which inspired Go-Daigo to return from exile and try again. The siege of Chihaya also inspired other samurai leaders to join Go-Daigo rather than the seemingly ineffective Hojo *bakufu*. The most important recruit was a warrior called Ashikaga Takauji, who was sent from Kamakura to recapture Go-Daigo, and ended up joining him. He showed his loyalty to his new master by attacking Kyoto and burning the *bakufu* headquarters there. This meant that Go-Daigo could return and become emperor again, and that the Hojo *shikken* rule was now confined to the distant city of Kamakura.

The Fall of Kamakura

Go-Daigo now needed a warrior family in the East to respond to his call and take up the war directly against the *bakufu*, and such a man was found in the person of a certain Nitta Yoshisada (1301–38). The Nitta were descended from Minamoto Yoshishige, whose descendants had settled in Kozuke province and taken as their surname the name of the locality. Nitta

Yoshisada had served in the Hojo army and had had the experience of pitting himself and his men against Kusunoki's mountain strongholds. His reasons for joining Go-Daigo were different from Kusunoki's. Unlike the Kusunoki the Nitta had not been tenants of imperial-owned lands for centuries, owing allegiance to the emperor as to an ordinary feudal lord. The Nitta were related to the Ashikaga, whose member, Takauji, had destroyed the *bakufu* in Kyoto, but were regarded as being of inferior status despite being descended from a senior branch of the Minamoto. This was

because their ancestor, at the time of the Gempei War, had committed the unforgivable sin: he had failed to respond to Yoritomo's call to arms. As a result he had not benefited from Yoritomo's generosity in the same way as other families, notably the Hojo, who were to become the regency. There were, therefore, sound reasons for the Nitta's disliking the Hojo, but few reasons were needed for supporting Go-Daigo other than to raise the Nitta to a prominent position by correctly supporting the eventual winner this time.

Nitta's defection to the imperial side came in 1333, shortly after receiving a *bakufu* summons to continue the siege of Chihaya. By now both Go-Daigo and his son, Prince Morinaga, were openly courting him. So by sending messages on ahead to other Minamoto vassals in his home province and neighbouring Kai, Shinano and Echigo, whom he knew would support him, Nitta Yoshisada was able to return to Kozuke in June 1333 and proclaim his rebellion in front of the Ikushima Shrine. Here he gathered his allies, and marched into Musashi. It was soon obvious that he intended to attack Kamakura directly, so the Hojo regent, Takatoki, sent a force to meet him, which engaged Nitta as he was attempting to cross the Tamagawa.

Our main source for the advance to Kamakura, as it is for the whole of the *Nambokucho-jidai*, the 'time of war between the courts', is the *Taiheiki*, an epic similar in style to *Heike Monogatari*. After a fierce fight, at which the Hojo first gained the upper hand, the position was reversed and the *bakufu* soldiers retreated into Kamakura with the Imperialists in hot pursuit. Nitta Yoshisada divided his forces into three divisions to attack from the north, east and west. The defenders likewise concentrated their efforts on the major entrances to the city, as:

North: Kewaizaka Pass, defended by Kanazawa Aritoki.

West: Gokuraku-ji Pass, defended by Daibutsu Sadanao.

East: Nagoe Pass, defended by Akahashi Moritoki.

The numbers of defenders are given as 30,000, 50,000 and 60,000 respectively, with 10,000 in reserve, held centrally in Kamakura. Perhaps if these figures are divided by

1333
THE BATTLE OF KAMAKURA

1333
THE BATTLE OF KAMAKURA

Right: Skull from Zaimokuza. This skull was excavated from Zaimokuza, site of some of the fiercest fighting in Kamakura. It bears a cut which has resulted from a thrust with the point of a sword, the *boshi*. (This photograph was kindly supplied by Dr Myra Shackley of Leicester University).

Right: Another skull from Zaimokuza. Another of the skulls studied for battle damage. This one has a series of chips where the edge of a sword has glanced off it. (This photograph was kindly supplied by Dr. Myra Shackley of Leicester University).

ten we may get an approximation of the actual numbers.

There were heavy casualties among the Hojo samurai on the north and the east, and many deeds of bravery which the *Taiheiki* describes in great detail, but after hours of fierce fighting no real breakthrough had been achieved, particularly on the western flank where the Gokuraku-ji Pass was held as firmly as ever. The pass was completely shut off with rows of stout wooden shields. Nitta Yoshisada went there himself to take a closer look, and realized that there was a chance of bypassing Gokuraku-ji altogether if it were possible to round the cape where the promontory of Inamuragasaki projects into the sea. There was a small expanse of beach at low tide, but the tide was then high, and the Hojo had taken the added precaution of floating several ships a short distance from the shore, from which a barrage of arrows covered any flanking attack.

At this point occurred the great legend of the Battle of Kamakura. This is how the *Taiheiki* tells it, in McCullough's translation: 'He dismounted from his horse, stripped off his helmet, and fell down and worshipped the sea, praying to the dragon-gods with all his might:

'I have heard that the Sun-Goddess of Ise, the founder of the land of Japan, conceals her true being in the august image of Vairocana Buddha, and that she has appeared in this world in the guise of a dragon-god of the blue ocean. Now her descendant our Emperor drifts on the waves of the western seas, oppressed by rebellious subjects . . . Let the eight dragon-gods of the inner and outer seas look upon my loyalty; let them roll back the tides a myriad leagues distant to open a way for my hosts.'

So he prayed, and cast his gold-mounted sword into the sea. May it not be that the dragon-gods accepted it? At the setting of the moon that night, suddenly for more than two thousand yards the waters ebbed away from Inamura Cape, where for the first time a broad flat beach appeared. Likewise the thousands of warships deployed to shoot flanking arrows were carried away with the running tide, until they floated far out on the sea. How strange it was! Never was such a thing as this!'

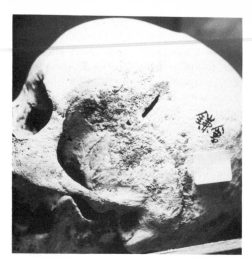

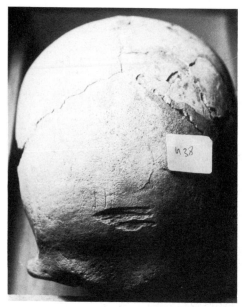

This account can of course be totally explained by the tide receding naturally, as it must have done, though the *Taiheiki* insists quite firmly that there was never a beach there before.

Once the imperialist troops were in the city the battle became a fierce hand-to-hand struggle among the burning houses, as the *bakufu* forces were torn between holding the passes and resisting the new advance round the cape. The *Taiheiki* is driven to use Hindu and Buddhist cosmology to convey to its readers the horror of the fighting as the Imperialists swept across Wakamiya Avenue: 'Fires were lighted among the commoners' houses along the beach, and also east and west of the Inase River, wherefrom flames like carriage wheels flew and scattered in black smoke . . . Entering clamorously beneath the fierce flames, the warriors of the Genji (i.e., the Imperialists) everywhere shot the bewildered enemy with arrows, cut them down with their swords, grappled with them, and stabbed them . . . Surely even thus was the battle of Indra's palace, when the *asuras* fell on to the swords and halberds, punished by the ruler of heaven! Even thus is the plight of sinners in the Hell of Constant Scorching, who sink to the bottom of the molten iron, driven by gaolers' whips!'

The fierceness of the battle, and the numbers employed of non-samurai troops, who were poorly supplied with defensive armour, have recently come to light with the excavation and analysis of grave pits in the Zaimokuza area of Kamakura, a district near the sea where the Hojo made their last stand. There used to be a bridge here known appropriately as *midare-bashi*, or 'confusion bridge'. Many skulls and fragments of weapons have been found, which have been studied by archaeologists. The pattern of wounds to the head indicate that none of the victims wore much in the way of head protection, which inclines one to the view that these grave pits were mass burial grounds for the common soldiers, while the samurai were buried elsewhere.

1333
THE BATTLE OF KAMAKURA

Left: Hara-kiri Cave. This cave, all that remains of the Tosho-ji temple, was the site of the mass suicide of the last members of the Hojo *shikken* when Kamakura fell.

1333
THE BATTLE OF KAMAKURA

Right: The Kuon-ji. This temple was found by Nitta Yoshisada as a temple of repose for those who were killed at the Battle of Kamakura. It is near the sea in the Zaimokusa district.

In fact, there has long been a tradition that samurai victims were interred in burial caves in the hills. The local rock is quite soft, hence the passes of Kamakura, and there are fifty or so such burial niches in the walls of the Shakado Tunnel, which was cut through a hill leading to the north-east of Kamakura in about 1250. One can still walk through it today, because motor traffic is now banned so as to prevent further damage to the walls. It must have seen much fierce fighting as the Imperialists broke in from the north. The tradition of victims of the battle being buried here was confirmed in 1965 when a landslip revealed a tombstone bearing the very date, 10 July 1333, when the city fell to Nitta Yoshisada.

When the battle was seen to be lost, the leaders of the Hojo *shikken* withdrew from their positions and retired to a temple called the Tosho-ji, a rather ironic name which means 'The temple of the victory in the East'. Here they committed suicide in the privacy of a cave behind the temple. Suicide by cutting open the abdomen, the well-known act of *hara-kiri*, was a deed of bravery admirable in a samurai who knew he was defeated, disgraced, or mortally wounded. The temple no longer exists, but 'hara-kiri' cave' is still there, and although

sited in a remote wooded spot on the fringe of the city, still attracts pilgrims. It is rare to visit it and not see fresh flowers as an offering.

Thus ended the Hojo regency, and the dominance of Kamakura. Within a few years a new dynasty of shoguns had been established from among the men who served Go-Daigo. But this family, the Ashikaga, returned to Kyoto to rule, leaving Kamakura as the historic 'former capital' it is today, and the site of a glorious and decisive battle.

Kamakura today

Kamakura is about an hour by train from Tokyo, and makes a pleasant contrast with that teeming city. It is a very popular tourist haunt, and everything is very easy to visit and enjoy. The places associated with the battle are not difficult to find, and as they are somewhat off the beaten track, (which runs unremittingly from the Great Buddha to the Tsurugaoka Hachiman and back), offer a pleasant and quiet stroll. The course of the attacks on the various passes can be followed with ease, and the discerning visitor is recommended to use Father Michael Cooper's guide *Exploring Kamakura*.

1560

The Battle of Okehazama

The battles of the Gempei and Nambokucho Wars set the standard by which samurai valour and military skill were judged, and there was little change in equipment or tactics over the next two centuries. Wars were still fought by samurai armed with bows and swords, supported by footsoldiers. The guerrilla-type warfare of the Nambokucho War saw much more fighting on foot than from horseback, but mounted samurai could still be used in devasting charges when conditions were appropriate.

With the *sengoku-jidai*, the 'Age of the Country at War', we see a completely new style of samurai warfare developing. This age, which roughly covers the sixteenth century, is dominated by three factors. First, the authority of the shogun has collapsed, so that wars are waged by clan against clan. Second, the battles are fought on an increasingly larger scale, with lower-class troops, the *ashigaru* ('light-feet') coming much more into prominence, and thirdly, from the mid 1540s onwards, we read of firearms being used for the first time in Japanese history.

The Battle of Okehazama, which I have chosen to introduce these rapid developments, has a number of interesting features: it was one of Oda Nobunaga's finest victories, made the more remarkable because it was won by a small force against one considerably larger, at odds of probably twelve to one; for one of the defeated commanders it was an engagement more profitable than most of his later victories; and finally, Okehazama, in common with several other battles in world history, (Hastings, for example), was not fought at the place which bears its name, but at a place called Dengaku-hazama, and given the name of Okehazama because that hamlet was the nearest habitation.

The Great Road

Okehazama and Dengaku-hazama are now almost swallowed up on the southern outskirts of one of Japan's largest modern cities, Nagoya, which borders the Pacific Ocean about 100 miles east of Osaka. The location of the battle gives a clue to the circumstances of the conflict. It lies on the narrow strip of land where the mountains of central Japan sweep down to the sea to form one of the great alluvial plains of Japan, the Nobi Plain. The land is crossed by several rivers, and since ancient times has been the course of the Tokaido, the 'Eastern Sea Road' which was one of the two roads linking central Japan (where the capital, Kyoto, was situated) with the eastern half of the country. The importance of the Tokaido in Japanese history cannot be overestimated. The mountainous Naka-sendo, the only practical alternative route, was prone to adverse weather in winter, so it is not surprising that the Tokaido has always been the main artery of Japan, and the site of several battles. In this book three conflicts: Okehazama, Mikata-ga-Hara and Sekigahara, happen either on or near the Tokaido, and all involve some degree of control of this vital link.

The gorge of Dengaku-hazama, where the fighting took place, is just off the old route of the Tokaido. Where Nagoya now sits were ricefields, a flat, muddy sea shore where bamboo grass and reeds waved in the breeze, and at least one very important Shinto shrine, Atsuta jinja, which still exists. Atsuta is among the holiest places of Japan's indigenous religion of Shinto, as it houses the Sacred Sword, one of the three items which go to make up the Japanese Imperial Regalia. The sword has been at Atsuta since AD 400, and was still being guarded by the priests when the armies rode past to Okehazama.

Today Nagoya is the chief city of the Prefecture of Aichi. Before the reform of local government in the last century Aichi consisted of the two provinces of Owari and Mikawa. Owari was the territory belonging to Oda Nobunaga, and Mikawa (along with Totomi and Suruga, further east

1560
THE BATTLE OF OKEHAZAMA

Right: Suit of armour. This suit of armour, from a private collection, is of *do-maru* style and bears many features typical of the period covered by the battles of the sixteenth century. It is of basically simple construction, with the minimum of decoration. Note how the armour plates are laced together in *kebiki-odoshi* style, with the dark-blue cords closely spaced, an arrangement repeated on the *haidate* (thigh guards) and the *sode* (shoulder guards). The *kote* (sleeve armour) are of mail on a cloth backing. The helmet bears the decoration of a grinning devil-face and horns.

Far left: Oda Nobunaga. This statue of Oda Nobunaga, victor of Okehazama, stands on the site of Kiyosu Castle, which was Nobunaga's base until his army captured Gifu. It was from Kiyosu that he set out to meet the Imagawa army at Okehazama. Little else remains of this vitally important fortress, as Japan's famous 'bullet train' goes through the middle of it!

Left: Imagawa Yoshimoto. Imagawa Yoshimoto (1519–60), general, administrator and aesthete, the first of the great *daimyo* to attempt a march on Kyoto, is chiefly remembered nowadays for being the general defeated by Nobunaga at the Battle of Okehazama (1560). This painted wooden statue of Imagawa Yoshimoto is in the Ieyasukan at Okazaki.

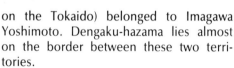

on the Tokaido) belonged to Imagawa Yoshimoto. Dengaku-hazama lies almost on the border between these two territories.

The Three Clans

The Battle of Okehazama involved three very important men: Oda Nobunaga, who won, Imagawa Yoshimoto, who lost, and Matsudaira Motoyasu, who was on the losing side but gained immeasurably from the defeat. As Okehazama is the first of three victories gained by Oda Nobunaga to be discussed in this book, it is worth devoting some time to an examination of the early life of this remarkable man, and the relationship between his family and the other two families involved.

The Oda family could trace its descent back to the Taira, the family defeated in the Gempei War, which was not usually a lineage that one shouted from the rooftops.

It does not appear greatly to have hindered their progress, and the Oda reached their threshold of destiny with Nobunaga's father, Oda Nobuhide. He witnessed the ruin of his overlords, the Shiba, following the Onin War of 1467–77, and occupied half of Owari province for his own family. Oda Nobunaga, his second son, was born in 1534.

There could not be a greater contrast between adversaries as that between Oda Nobunaga and the man he was to overcome at Okehazama, Imagawa Yoshimoto. The Imagawa were of impeccably ancient lineage, and actually descended from the Minamoto, who won the great Gempei War, which no doubt gave them an edge over their neighbours, the Oda. Among the family members was the great fourteenth-century author and historian, Imagawa Ryoshun, and in 1396 a certain Imagawa Norimasa was named *fuku-shogun* or

1560
THE BATTLE
OF OKEHAZAMA

'Deputy Shogun'. This Norimasa's great-great-grandson was Imagawa Yoshimoto (1519–60), who by 1560 ruled three provinces, and kept state in his capital of Sumpu (now Shizuoka) as if it were a miniature version of the capital. In fact a conscious attempt was made to make Sumpu into a little Kyoto, with gardens and palaces built and named after beauty spots in the capital, where Yoshimoto entertained leading *daimyo* and courtiers with supreme elegance.

Okehazama is often presented as if it were the first clash of arms between the Oda and the Imagawa. Although they were great rivals, fighting between them was rare until the early sixteenth century because their territories were separated by the domains of another – the Matsudaira family. In 1542 the Oda and the Imagawa met at Azuki-zaka, near Okazaki, the

Matsudaira capital, and Oda Nobuhide defeated Imagawa Yoshimoto. In that same year a son was born to the Matsudaira *daimyo*, Hirotada, who was to grow up to be the famous Tokugawa Ieyasu, the future shogun. The samurai class were always changing names, and at the time of Okehazama this young man was called Matsudaira Motoyasu. From the year of his birth this Motoyasu's fortunes were to be bound up in the destinies of the Imagawa and Oda.

As noted above the Matsudaira were based at Okazaki, a pleasant castle town on the Tokaido in Mikawa province. Relations with the Oda, whose territory theirs touched, were never good, and there were many skirmishes. In 1548 Oda Nobuhide, Nobunaga's father, sent an army against Okazaki, apparently as a revenge attack following the failure of a clever scheme to seduce one of the Matsudaira clansmen

into surrendering a certain castle. Faced by a huge army pouring down the Tokaido towards Okazaki, Matsudaira Hirotada asked for help from the *daimyo* in the next province along – who was of course Imagawa Yoshimoto. Yoshimoto agreed to help, but in the custom of the times asked for a hostage as guarantee of good behaviour, the idea being that such a hostage would have his throat cut at the least sign of rebellion. The hostage was to be the six-year-old Motoyasu, who was sent from Okazaki with as much dignity as his beleaguered father could muster. But Motoyasu never reached his destination. On the way to the Imagawa capital of Sumpu his procession was intercepted, Motoyasu was kidnapped, and became instead a hostage of the Oda.

With their heir captive the Matsudaira fortunes declined as the Imagawa and the

Oda fought around them. In 1548 Imagawa Yoshimoto gained revenge on Oda Nobuhide by defeating him in a second battle at Azuki-zaka, and the following year Oda Nobuhide died. Imagawa Yoshimoto (or rather his uncle, Sessai Choro, a Zen monk who led his army for him), followed up this fortuitous death by besieging Nobuhide's sons, Nobuhiro and Nobunaga, in the castle of Anjo, which was only spared when they agreed to hand over the hostage, Motoyasu. So Motoyasu finally arrived at Sumpu three years late.

Matsudaira Motoyasu lived in the comfortable 'prison' of Sumpu until he was fifteen, when he performed his *gembuku*, the ceremony of manhood. In 1555 Imagawa Yoshimoto lost his redoubtable uncle, the Zen monk, and things did not look so promising for the Imagawa, as Yoshimoto was weak without his guidance. But the young Motoyasu was to prove a capable solider. He fought his first battle in 1558, which gave him a taste of action on the border between Mikawa and Oda Nobunaga's Owari.

Around the border area, where Okehazama was shortly to flare into prominence in Japanese history, were half a dozen or so forts, which are shown in the map on page 37. The term castle conjures up too grand a picture of these structures. They were fairly typical *yamashiro*, (mountain castles), or *hirajiro* (plain castles), which took advantage of any natural surroundings, with added moats, walls made of a clay plaster on a reed background, watch-towers and domestic quarters. Very little stone would have been used in their construction, as is indicated by the frequent references to such forts being burned. They appear to have changed hands quite regularly, and it was one such defection in 1558 that led to Motoyasu's first taste of action.

A fort called Terabe, held for the Imagawa by one Suzuki Shigeteru, had been surrendered to Nobunaga. As Mikawa was theoretically Motoyasu's ancestral territory Imagawa Yoshimoto dispatched him to retake it. He was seventeen years old and led the attack in person. They burned the outer defence works, but observed that there were several subsidiary forts from which they could easily be taken in the rear

1560
THE BATTLE
OF OKEHAZAMA

1560
THE BATTLE
OF OKEHAZAMA

Right: Dengaku-hazama. The Battle of Okehazama was fought in this wooded gorge called Dengakuhazama. Here Yoshimoto had rested during his advance, and here he was caught by Nobunaga's surprise attack.

if their attention were held for too long by the main fortress. So Motoyasu set fire to the main stronghold and withdrew. The expected rear attack came soon after, but Motoyasu was ready for it and drove Nobunaga's men away with considerable loss to the Oda.

In order to carry out this operation Motoyasu had collected his own, Matsudaira, clan army from Okazaki, and not unnaturally this led to demands from the Matsudaira to have Motoyasu returned to them permanently. But this enthusiastic and skilled samurai was too useful for Imagawa to give him up, and he was to prove his worth again the following year, in a well-conducted little operation called the 'provisioning of Odaka'. Odaka was another of the frontier forts and, as the map shows, protected the Imagawa left flank against the sea. It had originally been constructed by Nobunaga, but, like Terabe, had been surrendered to the other side. Its position therefore put it some way into Nobunaga's territory, and it had not proved difficult to isolate it from Mikawa. The blockade, controlled from the forts of Washizu and Marune, which surrounded it, was succeeding admirably when Motoyasu came on the scene.

Motoyasu decided to cover the run for Odaka by a complex diversionary attack. A glance at the map shows the relationship between the various forts. Motoyasu sent 1,000 men against Terabe and Umezu in the middle of the night, and waited patiently with about 800 men who were guarding the baggage train. His army was under orders to make as much noise as possible during the attacks on Terabe and Umezu, and soon the noise of the fighting in the forts, and the crackle and explosion of burning wood, reached the ears of the defenders of Washizu and Marune, who immediately sent almost their entire garrisons to the succour of their comrades. Motoyasu then led 1,200 pack-animals straight into Odaka, under the eyes of the frustrated defenders who were too few in number to do anything about it.

The March to Okehazama
During the following year Motoyasu was occupied in similar endeavours on Imagawa Yoshimoto's behalf, all of which were the

preliminaries to Imagawa's decisive move, for Imagawa Yoshimoto was destined to be the first of the great *daimyo* to attempt a march on Kyoto, the capital of Japan. This was the great dream of all the *daimyo*, that one day they could rise beyond mere local control to taking over the then powerless shogunate. Some clans, such as the Takeda and the Uesugi, were hampered by geography, but the Imagawa domains lay along the main road of Japan, and all that stood between Imagawa and Kyoto was the upstart Oda Nobunaga, whom his faithful Motoyasu had twice outsmarted in the past year. Yoshimoto simply could not lose.

In June 1560 Yoshimoto assembled all the forces of Mikawa, Totomi and Suruga, including all of Motoyasu's Matsudaira troops, into one gigantic army of possibly 25,000 men. The border forts, so bitterly contested for two decades, were the first objective. Imagawa held two: Odani, which thanks to Motoyasu had held out, and Narumi, which was very strategically placed on the Tokaido itself. Oda Nobunaga also controlled two main forts: Washizu and Marune, whose garrisons had been embarrassed at the provisioning of Odaka, and three other minor structures. Leaving these alone for the present, the Imagawa samurai attacked Washizu while their Matsudaira comrades attacked Marune.

The latter was a hard-fought victory. At first Motoyasu launched a sharp attack,

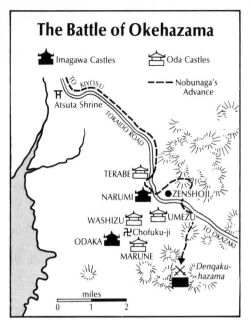

The Battle of Okehazama

- 🏯 Imagawa Castles
- ⛩ Oda Castles
- --- Nobunaga's Advance

TO KIYOSU
Atsuta Shrine
TOKAIDO ROAD
TERABE
NARUMI ● ZENSHOJI
WASHIZU UMEZU
TO OKAZAKI
ODAKA 卍 Chofuku-ji
MARUNE
Denqaku-hazama

miles
0 1 2

Noh play *Atsumori*, which deals with the death at the Battle of Ichinotani of Taira Atsumori, from whose clan the Oda were descended. He then put on his armour, had breakfast, and left Kiyosu with little more than 200 men. Forerunners rallied his retainers through Owari, and by the time he reached the Atsuta Shrine his army had grown to about 2,000. Here he wrote a prayer for victory, which he deposited with the priest, then rode off to meet Imagawa. The Shinto priests remarked that his demeanour was such that he did not look as if he were going into a battle. Indeed, he was cool to the point of abstraction, sitting side-saddle and humming a tune.

By the time he reached the border area Washizu and Marune had fallen, and the smoke was still rising from the burning buildings in the distance. He halted a short way before Imagawa's fortress of Narumi on the Tokaido, and sent out scouts to get an up-to-date picture of the situation. They reported that Washizu and Marune were destroyed and that Matsudaira Motoyasu's army had rested in Odaka, but that the vast bulk of the Imagawa army, including the commander-in-chief himself, had chosen to rest in a wooded gorge called Dengaku-hazama, where they were celebrating their victories in some style. It was territory Nobunaga knew well, and provided the perfect opportunity for a surprise attack.

First he had to assure Imagawa that no such move was being planned, so with much ado took up a position at Zenshoji, quite near to Imagawa's fort of Narumi, and directly in line with Dengaku-hazama. Here his army rigged up a very impressive dummy army. This was not as difficult as it sounds, because a Japanese army in those days always carried hundreds of long vertical banners called *nobori*, and it was customary for samurai to wear a small flag, the *sashimono*, on the backs of their armour. The nature of the Japanese countryside also lends itself towards such duplicity. Japanese hills do not roll like English ones. They rise up suddenly from the flatlands, so it was easy for Nobunaga to select an appropriate hill and cover its summit, just behind the brow, with the insignia of a considerable host, as Yoshinaka had done at Kurikara. (Admirers of the Japanese cinema will also recall a similar

then withdrew. The garrison most unwisely pursued them to where Motoyasu had prepared a position and had assembled a large number of arquebuses and bows. As the Oda samurai attacked, Motoyasu poured bullets and arrows into them. One bullet brought down the fort's commander. Pleased by this achievement Imagawa Yoshimoto congratulated Motoyasu and suggested that he rest his men within Odaka. It was a fateful suggestion, because it enabled Motoyasu's army to avoid the terrible destiny that was in store for his overlord.

As Washizu had also fallen there was no evidence at that time of any dark fate awaiting the Imagawa. Everything was going their way. They could now mask the small Oda forts and move on along the Tokaido a further twelve miles to Oda Nobunaga's capital of Kiyosu, which their huge army would take with ease. Even the reports that Nobunaga was advancing to meet them caused no alarm. His army was so small compared to their own that the risk was entirely discounted.

Nobunaga's Advance
Nobunaga had been warned the previous night that Marune and Washizu were under attack from a colossal Imagawa army. He had appeared unconcerned when the messages arrived, but rose early the following morning and chanted a few lines from the

37

trick beautifully illustrated in Akira Kurosawa's film *Ran*.)

The Battle of Okehazama

As Nobunaga was operating on home ground it was also an easy operation to lead 3,000 men on a circular route through the wooded hills behind Zenshoji, to drop down behind Dengaku-hazama from the north. Even the weather was on his side. It was a stifling hot day, and Yoshimoto's sentries were not at their most alert. *Noh* choruses were being chanted as Imagawa Yoshimoto performed the traditional ceremony of viewing the heads of the enemy. One by one the grisly trophies were paraded in front of him, a label on the pig-tail proclaiming the names of the victim and the noble samurai who had defeated him. Food was consumed, and the *sake* flowed freely, as Yoshimoto, dressed in an elaborate suit of armour, declared to his men that neither god or demon dared to meet his army.

At about midday on 22 June 1560, as Nobunaga's men drew silently near, a terrific thunderstorm began, which cloaked Nobunaga's final movements as Imagawa's men huddled under trees from the torrential rain. As the clouds blew away, the Oda troops poured into the gorge of Dengaku-hazama. The Imagawa troops were so unprepared for an attack that they fled in all directions, leaving Yoshimoto's curtained field headquarters quite unprotected. Imagawa Yoshimoto was unaware of what was happening; he thought that a drunken fight had broken out among his men, and seeing an angry-looking samurai running towards him barked out an order for the man to return to his post. He did not realize that this was one of Nobunaga's men until the samurai thrust a spear at him, but by then it was too late. He drew his sword and cut through the shaft of the spear, the blade continuing in a wide sweep to cut the attacker's knee, but before he could do any more a second samurai grabbed him and lopped off his head. He was 41 years old, an accomplished aesthete and administrator, and he died a samurai's death.

Many others of the Imagawa army died a samurai's death. In one of a collection of articles about the battle, Hayashi Ryosho (1983) and other authors give a full list of combatants of samurai rank. Sixty named samurai appear in the list of followers of Oda Nobunaga, of whom six are listed as 'killed in action', and none as wounded. On the Imagawa side, of the *honjin*, the 'headquarters unit' present in the gorge with Yoshimoto, sixty-two samurai are named and all but two were killed. Of the large number of Mikawa men who served under Matsudaira Motoyasu in the attack on Marune, the casualties are as negligible as those of the Oda side.

That was the pattern of Okehazama. With their leader dead the mighty Imagawa army melted away or was cut down. Matsudaira Motoyasu was one of the first to be told of his death, and refused to believe it, but his retainers urged him to withdraw from

Marune in case Nobunaga's victorious army turned its full weight against them. Prudent as ever, he sent a runner to Dengaku-hazama to confirm the news, and then pulled his samurai back to Okazaki.

For the first time in his life Motoyasu was free of the Imagawa. Yoshimoto had a son, Ujizane, waiting nervously in Sumpu, for he was no soldier, but Motoyasu felt no obligation towards a born loser. Instead Motoyasu waited patiently outside Okazaki in the temple of Daiju-ji, the Matsudaira's family temple, until it was clear that the Imagawa retainers had retreated into Totomi and Suruga provinces, then entered his ancestral capital to claim it as his own. He had shared in a defeat, but only Nobunaga got more out of the victory.

Over the next decade, abandoned by his father's allies, Imagawa Ujizane's empire crumbled under the attacks of avaricious neighbours. Incredibly, he lived to a ripe old age, having survived some of the most tumultuous years of Japan's history. He became a monk and died aged 77 at Edo in 1614. A born loser he may have been, but Ujizane was one of nature's survivors.

Okehazama Today

The skill in visiting the Okehazama battle site lies in locating Dengaku-hazama, rather than the 'official' battle memorial, which is not in the correct place! Take the Meitetsu Nagoya Railway line from Nagoya, which goes on to Okazaki. Alight at Arimatsu. (The station name is written only in Jap-

1560
THE BATTLE OF OKEHAZAMA

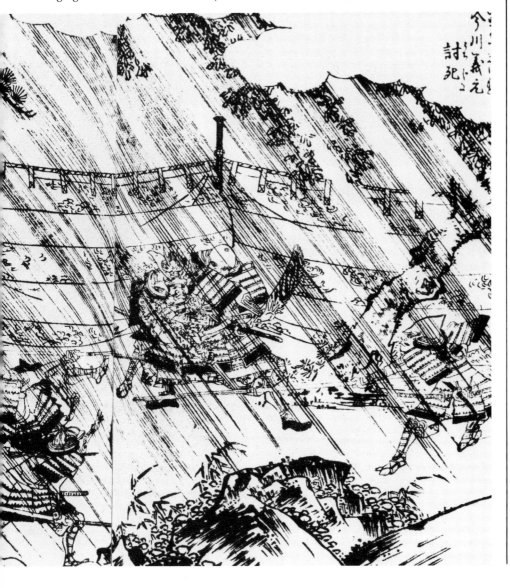

Left: The death of Imagawa Yoshimoto. Taking advantage of a sudden thunderstorm, Nobunga's small force attacked Yoshimoto's encampment at Dengaku-hazama. Imagawa Yoshimoto was surrounded and killed.

二

1560
THE BATTLE
OF OKEHAZAMA

Right: The headmound of the Chofuku-ji. The heads of the defeated Imagawa samurai were piled here, and later buried. The Chofuku-ji honours their memories. The stone bears an inscription referring to the Battle of Okehazama.

anese). From Arimatsu it is best to take a taxi. When the author visited the site in 1986 there was some building work going on nearby which appears to have taken much of Dengaku-hazama with it, though the pool from which Imagawa Yoshimoto drank is still there. There is a memorial stone, and a notice-board confirming (in English) that you have the right place! Even though so little is left of the site, it has a strange atmosphere about it, which is added to by the overgrown and dilapidated little Shinto shrine in the copse. No other battlefield has such an eerie presence.

A short distance away is the temple of Chofuku-ji where the heads are buried. The enthusiast may also visit the sites of the fortresses of Marune and Washizu, which are marked by memorials, but nothing else. The ruins of Kiyosu Castle are now a park, but the New Tokaido Line runs right through it! There is, however, a fine statue of Nobunaga on the mound. Okazaki, further down the line from Okehazama, is much more rewarding. The castle has been rebuilt, and there are several monuments and statues associated with Ieyasu, including the splendid Ieyasukan museum.

1561

The Fourth Battle of Kawanakajima

Deep in the heart of the mountain range known as the Japan Alps is a wide plain where the Chikumagawa and Saigawa rivers meet. This plain, Kawanakajima, 'the island between the rivers' was the site of no less than five 'Battles of Kawanakajima', fought between the same two samurai clans, the Takeda and the Uesugi.

When one examines the geography of this part of Japan it is not surprising that Kawanakajima should have become a battleground. The area is flat, and well served by communications from the valleys that lead down from the surrounding mountains. It had long been fertile land (today it is a centre of fruit growing and market gardening) and therefore a rich prize for any samurai warlord. Most important of all, in the mid sixteenth century Kawanakajima was where the recognized territories of the Uesugi (Lords of Echigo province), and the Takeda (Lords of Kai province), actually met. As a result it witnessed conflict between the two families as 'Battles of Kawanakajima', in 1553, 1555, 1557, 1561 and 1564.

It is the fourth of these battles that is usually indicated by the phrase 'The Battle of Kawanakajima', but in fact all the five conflicts have been much neglected by non-Japanese historians. If they are mentioned at all beside the exploits of Oda Nobunaga and Tokugawa Ieyasu, the struggles at Kawanakajima are often relegated to the status of mock battles, where large numbers of troops were placed in position, only for one side to withdraw politely once a theoretical tactical or strategic advantage had been gained. Notwithstanding the fact that several of these battles had indecisive results owing to the prudence of the commanders, who chose to withdraw to fight again, the battles at Kawanakajima were anything but mock. In fact the Fourth Battle of Kawanakajima, as we shall see, was fought in deadly earnest and produced a very high percentage of casualties on both sides. It also gave Japan some of its most

enduring samurai legends, and some of its archetypal heroes. These battles also gave an opportunity for new warlords like Oda Nobunaga to assert themselves, as for a decade the Takeda and the Uesugi were obsessed with fighting each other and ignored the rest of Japan.

There are few written records for any of these battles except the fourth, in 1561, and even for this our main source is an epic called the *Koyo Gunkan*, a chronicle of the Takeda family, whose authorship is attributed to Kosaka Danjo Masanobu, one of Takeda Shingen's lifelong retainers and a veteran of at least one of the five battles. The *Koyo Gunkan* is supposed to have been written soon after the event. It is written in epic style, but fits in with other descriptions, with oral tradition, and with local topography.

Takeda Shingen

To understand the background to this bitterly fought five-round contest let us examine the two contenders: Uesugi Kenshin and Takeda Shingen, for the battles at Kawanakajima are essentially contests between these two very powerful men. Both were *daimyo*, great landowners, who ruled their provinces completely independently, and paid little heed to the nominal central government of the shogun.

The Takeda were an ancient family descended from Minamoto Yoshimitsu (1056–1127), brother of the celebrated hero, Minamoto Yoshiie, and Yoshimitsu's son, Yoshikiyo, was the first to take the surname of Takeda. His grandson, Takeda Nobuyoshi (1138–86), supported Minamoto Yoritomo, the leader of the Minamoto clan, in the civil war of Gempei when the Minamoto fought the Taira. In 1192 the victorious Minamoto Yoritomo became the first shogun of Japan, and as a result of the Minamoto triumph the Takeda clan became very powerful in their part of Japan. When the Minamoto shoguns were supplanted by the Hojo, and then the Ashikaga in succeeding

41

1561
THE FOURTH BATTLE OF KAWANAKAJIMA

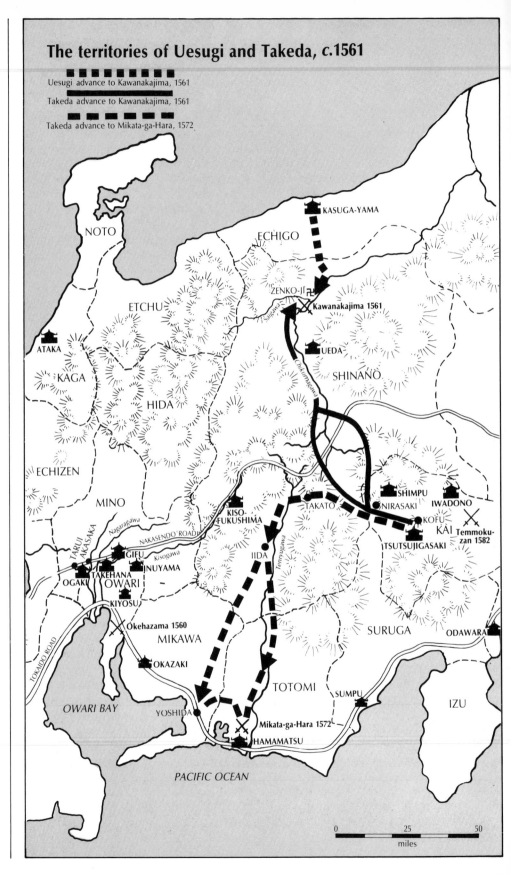

The territories of Uesugi and Takeda, *c.*1561

▪▪▪▪▪▪▪▪ Uesugi advance to Kawanakajima, 1561

▬▬▬▬▬▬ Takeda advance to Kawanakajima, 1561

▬ ▬ ▬ ▬ Takeda advance to Mikata-ga-Hara, 1572

KASUGA-YAMA

ECHIGO

NOTO

ETCHU

ZENKO-JI
Kawanakajima 1561

ATAKA

KAGA

UEDA

SHINANO

HIDA

ECHIZEN

MINO

KISO-
FUKUSHIMA

TAKATO

SHIMPU

NIRASAKI

IWADONO

KOFU

KAI   Temmoku-
zan 1582

TSUTSUJIGASAKI

TARUI
AKASAKA

NAKASENDO ROAD

IIDA

GIFU

INUYAMA

OGAKI

TAKEHANA

OWARI

KIYOSU

Okehazama 1560

MIKAWA

OKAZAKI

SURUGA

ODAWARA

OWARI BAY

YOSHIDA

TOTOMI

SUMPU

IZU

Mikata-ga-Hara 1572

HAMAMATSU

TOKAIDO ROAD

PACIFIC OCEAN

0   25   50
miles

42

centuries, the Takeda were recognized as governors of Kai Province under the shogun. When warfare put the centralized shogunate at a disadvantage the Takeda were but one of the many samurai clans that took advantage of the weakness of the Ashikaga shoguns to establish themselves as landowners and rulers in their own right. In the case of the Takeda, they managed to convert the governorship of the province of Kai into their own feudal territory, and Takeda Nobutora (1493–1573) established himself in 1519 as *daimyo* in his capital of Fuchu (now the city of Kofu).

This Nobutora was a considerable leader of samurai, but is best known for being the father of the famous Takeda Shingen, who was born in 1521. 'Shingen' was in fact the Buddhist name his son took on becoming a monk in 1551. Shingen (or Harunobu as he was then known) had received his baptism of fire in 1536, as the early age of fifteen. His father had attacked a certain Hiraga Genshin, who had opposed his moves to take over Kai, at Hiraga's fortress of Uminokuchi. Nobutora was forced to retreat, but the young Harunobu came to his rescue and soundly defeated the rival clan, giving early promise of a legendary military skill.

Some time after this, father and son were again under arms, but in opposition to each other, because Nobutora had resolved to disinherit Harunobu and pass his territory on to his younger son Nobushige, whom Nobutora particularly favoured. In 1540 Harunobu revolted, seized his father and

1561
THE FOURTH BATTLE OF KAWANAKAJIMA

Left: Takeda Shingen. Takeda Shingen (1521–73), wearing a *jinbaori* (surcoat) and a monk's *kesa* (scarf), rises from his camp-stool to parry with his war-fan the blows aimed at him by Uesugi Kenshin at the Fourth Battle of Kawanakajima.

placed him under the custody of his (Shingen's) father-in-law, Imagawa Yoshimoto, at his capital of Sumpu. With this act Harunobu took total control of Kai, and it is from 1540 onwards that a new expansionist Takeda begin to increase their influence into neighbouring territories. There were several conflicts with the Hojo, but from the point of view of the battles at Kawanakajima their most important sorties were to the north, towards the provinces of Shinano and Echigo.

In 1547 the Takeda invaded Shinano. Some *daimyo*, such as the Sanada, submitted to the Takeda and became vassals. Others resisted them to the last. The most important among the latter group was Murakami Yoshikiyo (1501–73), whom Shingen defeated in a bitter battle at Ueda-hara in 1548. He had fought against Shingen's father, but realized that he could not stand alone against the new power of Shingen, so he asked for help from his powerful neighbour to the north, Uesugi Kenshin. The resulting alliance between Murakami Yoshikiyo and Uesugi Kenshin thus brought these two powerful clans into direct opposition, and Kawanakajima was their testing-ground.

Uesugi Kenshin

Unlike Takeda Shingen's long pedigree, his adversary's social position, and indeed his name, owed everything to clever opportunism. There was indeed an ancient family of Uesugi that was descended from the Fujiwara, but the most illustrious samurai to bear the name, this Uesugi Terutora (like Shingen, 'Kenshin' was a Buddhist name adopted later in adult life) had no hereditary connection with the Uesugi line.

His original name was in fact Nagao Kagetora. The family of Nagao were retainers of the Yamanouchi branch of the Uesugi, and of some military reputation. But in 1545 the Uesugi were defeated by the Hojo clan. The defeated Uesugi leader, Uesugi Norimasa (1522–79), went from bad to worse in his campaigns against the Hojo until in 1551, defeated once again, by Hojo Ujiyasu, he was forced to seek refuge with his vassal Nagao Kagetora.

Kagetora had grown rich in the service of the Uesugi, and had become *de facto* ruler of Echigo Province, which bordered the Japan Sea coast, from his castle of Kasugayama. Echigo was a province of fertile ricefields, protected from the belligerent Hojo and Takeda by the 'Japan Alps'. When Uesugi came to him on bended knee he accepted his erstwhile overlord on his own very strict terms. Norimasa was to adopt him as his heir, give him the name of Uesugi and the titles of Echigo-no-kami 'Lord of Echigo' and Kanto Kanrei 'Shogun's Deputy for the Kanto area'. Norimasa agreed to all these demands, and Nagao Kagetora became Uesugi Terutora. He took the name of Kenshin in the following year, 1552. Kenshin's adoption into the Uesugi thus took place four years after Murakami Yoshikiyo had requested his help to repulse Shingen. He had supported the Murakami already as Nagao Kagetora, but it was as the newly created Uesugi Kenshin that he fought the First Battle of Kawanakajima.

The Early Battles

The principal role of any *daimyo* of the civil war period was to be a leader in war, and the armies of the great *daimyo* were as well organized as any other aspect of their princely responsibilities. Takeda Shingen and Uesugi Kenshin were prime examples of sensible division of labour and delegation of command, the latter functioning through a small core of trusted relatives and

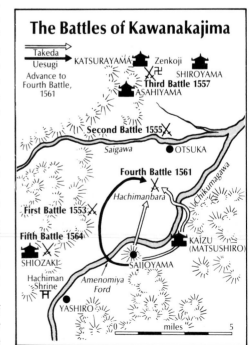

The Battles of Kawanakajima

Takeda
Uesugi
Advance to Fourth Battle, 1561

KATSURAYAMA   Zenkoji
SHIROYAMA
Third Battle 1557
ASAHIYAMA

Second Battle 1555

Saigawa   OTSUKA

Fourth Battle 1561

Hachimanbara

Chikumagawa

First Battle 1553

Fifth Battle 1564
SHIOZAKI

KAIZU (MATSUSHIRO)

SAIJOYAMA

Hachiman Shrine   Amenomiya Ford

YASHIRO

miles   5

close retainers. Takeda Shingen depended particularly upon his 'Twenty-Four Generals', some of whom were his relatives (including three brothers), some veterans of his father's campaigns, and others were taken on the strength because of outstanding personal qualities. A few, of whom the Sanada are the outstanding example, were defeated enemies made vassals.

Uesugi Kenshin had a similar, but slightly larger band known as the 'Twenty-Eight Generals'. Among them we note a member of the Nagao family, from which Kenshin had come, and allies treated on equal terms with the family (such as the unfortunate Murakami Yoshikiyo) and several others who were to make names for themselves at Kawanakajima.

A study of the historical records shows that Shingen and Kenshin actually met at Kawanakajima on seven occasions, of which only five are regarded as 'Battles of Kawanakajima'. The first three of these 'official' battles Kawanakajima between the rivals were indecisive, and may be regarded as preliminaries for the bloody encounter of 1561.

The map on page 44 shows the location of the early battles. The Kawanakajima plain is triangular in shape and surrounded on all sides by mountains. To the north of the plain the Saigawa flows almost due east,

and makes a natural northern boundary. The wider and stronger Chikumagawa flows from south-west to north-east, where it is joined by the Saigawa, skirting closely the southern mountain range, and thereby restricting an army's access to the plain from any southerly direction.

Just to the south of the Chikumagawa Takeda Shingen maintained a fortress, Kaizu Castle, an old place which he had rebuilt after the invasion of Shinano. Kaizu was the Takeda forward position against the Uesugi. North of the Saigawa, on the edge of the northern mountains, is the great Buddhist temple of Zenko-ji which was effectively a Uesugi possession, and is now surrounded by the modern city of Nagano. The history of the battles at Kawanakajima is therefore the story of two powerful clans at the limits of their geographical power, each territory being limited by the comparative safety of the two mountain ranges whose passes led to Kai and to Echigo. Kawanakajima was their no man's land, and their very rich prize.

The fighting began in 1553, and during this year they met on three occasions, of which a skirmish during the month of September is regarded as the 'First Battle of Kawanakajima'. In June of the same year Shingen had penetrated north into the Kawanakajima plain as far as the present-

1561
THE FOURTH BATTLE OF KAWANAKAJIMA

Left: The ruins of Kaizu Castle. Kaizu Castle, which now lies within the town of Matsushiro, marked the furthest point of Takeda influence into the plain of Kawanakajima, which lies just across the river Chikumagawa. All that is left of Shingen's fortress are the foundation walls.

1561
THE FOURTH BATTLE OF KAWANAKAJIMA

Right: The Saigawa. The Saigawa, seen here from the modern railway bridge, marks the northern boundary of the plain of Kawanakajima. The Second Battle of Kawanakajima was 'fought' across the Saigawa directly east of this position.

day town of Yashiro. Here his vanguard encountered the Uesugi army near a shrine to Hachiman, but disengaged. They came into conflict again a few miles to the north in the First Battle of Kawanakajima, otherwise known from its precise location as 'The Battle of Fuse'. Once again both sides avoided a decisive battle, but in October the Uesugi army defeated the Takeda as they withdrew past the Hachiman Shrine, the same site as the earlier skirmish.

The Second Battle of Kawanakajima, otherwise known as 'The Battle of the Saigawa', took place two years later when Shingen returned to the contest for Kawanakajima and advanced across the plain as far as the Saigawa. He occupied a hill called Otsuka just to the south of the river and made camp on it. Kenshin's army was based on a hill called Shiroyama ('castle hill') just east of the Zenkoji, a position which offered a commanding view of the Kawanakajima plain. But Kenshin did not completely control these northern hills, because a few miles to the west lay Asahiyama, on which was a castle of the same name that was controlled by a family known

as Kurita. The Kurita, who had some connection with the Zenko-ji, were sympathetic to the Takeda, and therefore menaced Kenshin's right flank. Shingen's force consisted of 3,000 men, of whom 800 were archers and 300 arquebusiers.

Eventually Kenshin responded to the challenge and led his army down to the Saigawa, where he arranged his samurai against Shingen on the northern bank. From August to November of 1555 both armies sat and waited for the other to make a move. In fact the sight of the two generals glaring at each other across the Saigawa is a popular theme found in later woodblock prints, where the Saigawa is depicted as a shallow stream, with both armies prepared for action. But there was little fighting, and the contest became one of political manoeuvring. Kenshin was faced with the defection from his allies of a retainer called Kitajo Takahiro, who held a strategically important castle, and eventually both armies pulled back to deal with such domestic affairs.

The third clash occurred in 1557. Shingen advanced into the northern part of Kawan-

akajima and, in his furthest penetration on to Uesugi territory, captured the mountain fortress of Katsurayama, which overlooked Zenko-ji from the north-west. He also launched a fierce attack against Iiyama Castle, to the north-east of the Zenko-ji along the road to Echigo province. Kenshin responded by a sortie from the Zenko-ji, where he had based his army, and Shingen withdrew, again avoiding a decisive battle.

The Fourth Battle of Kwanakajima

The Fourth Battle of Kawanakajima is 'the' Battle of Kawanakajima. It is one most usually depicted in works of art, and eclipsed in scale any encounter that had preceded it.

It is quite clear that Uesugi Kenshin was determined to fight a final and decisive battle. In mid September 1461 he left his headquarters of Kasugayama Castle at the head of 18,000 soldiers, determined to destroy Shingen once and for all. Kasugayama was a *yamashiro*, a mountain-top castle, quite close to the Japan Sea coast, near the present-day town of Takada, and about 45 miles due north of Kawanakajima.

His objective was Shingen's Kaizu Castle, just south of the Chikumagawa in the present-day town of Matsushiro. This time Kenshin did not make his base at the Zenko-ji, but decided to threaten Kaizu from nearer at hand, on high ground of his own choosing. So, leaving about a quarter of his troops in the Zenko-ji, Kenshin crossed the Saigawa and the Chikumagawa, and took up a position on Saijoyama, a mountain to the west of the castle, which forms a north-westerly pointing spur of the southern chain. Here his army looked down on Kaizu. He strengthened Saijoyama with field fortifications, and began to wait patiently for any move from the Kai army.

The Kaizu garrison, which numbered no more than 150 mounted samurai and their followers, appears to have been taken completely by surprise at Kenshin's move. They were under the command of Kosaka Danjo Masanobu, one of Shingen's Twenty-Four Generals, his lover and his closest companion. Kaizu was ninety miles from Tsutsujigasaki, Shingen's fortress in Kofu, but a well-organized system of signal-fires enabled Kosaka Danjo to transmit to his lord in less than two hours the news that Kenshin had advanced. Uesugi Kenshin made no attempt to prevent the message from getting through. His threat to Kaizu was merely the bait that would encourage Shingen to bring a large army to the foot of Saijoyama, where Kenshin could fall upon him.

The moment that Shingen received the signal he gave orders for the Kai-based army to mobilize. The position was very serious. His main fear was that Kenshin would take Kaizu, which controlled communications north on to the plain of Kawanakajima, and from Kawanakajima south through the mountain passes. For Shingen ever to succeed in his long war against Kenshin, Kaizu had to be held. Shingen took personal command of a host of 16,000 men. They marched in two sections, rejoining near Ueda, and continued north on the west bank of the Chikumagawa, which here flows in a northerly direction. No doubt divining Kenshin's intentions he kept the Chikumagawa on his right flank, always between him and Saijoyama, until he reached the ford of Amenomiya, where he pitched camp with

47

1561
THE FOURTH BATTLE OF KAWANAKAJIMA

Right: Saijoyama and the Chikumagawa. Looking across the Chikumagawa from the Kawanakajima side we see Saijoyama in the distance, site of Uesugi Kenshin's field camp prior to the Fourth Battle of Kawanaka- jima. It was near the modern bridge, from which the photograph was taken, that Shingen's army forded the river to take up a position at Hachimanbara.

Right: Kawanaka- jima. This view of the plain of Kawanaka- jima, taken from the west, shows how flat the area is compared to the surrounding hills. The modern bridge across the Chikumagawa (which on this stretch has altered its course considerably since 1561) marks the approximate posi- tion of the ford of Amenomiya, associ- ated with Amakasu Kagemochi's rear- guard struggle. Behind Amenomiya lies Saijoyama, the site of Kenshin's camp and Kosaka Danjo's night attack.

Left: Yamamoto Kansuke. The veteran of Shingen's army and his most trusted adviser, Yamamoto Kansuke, thought of the idea of 'Operation Woodpecker', and committed suicide when their opponent Kenshin's brilliant generalship caused it to fail. Kansuke was a Buddhist monk, and fought Kawanakajima, his final battle, at the age of 69. (His spectacular helmet is illustrated in the author's *Samurai Warriors*.)

the river between him and Kenshin's position. It had taken them 24 days to reach Kawanakajima.

The situation was similar to that which had come about during the Second Battle of Kawanakajima, when the two evenly balanced armies had faced each other across the Saigawa. Neither army made a move. Both knew that for a battle to succeed there had to be an element of surprise to throw the adversary off balance. Suddenly Shingen struck camp, crossed the Chikumagawa in front of Saijoyama, and marched his army straight into Kaizu. The numbers of his troops, swollen by reinforcements from Shinano, had by now grown to about 20,000, but this vast host were not to remain for long packed into the castle. Shingen, or rather his *gun-bugyo* ('Army Commissioner'), Yamamoto Kansuke, had plans.

Yamamoto Kansuke Haruyuki, to give him his full name, is one of the most interesting of Shingen's generals. He too had taken holy orders (like Shingen, Kansuke is a Buddhist name), and he is frequently represented wearing a white head cowl in place of his spectacular buffalo-horned helmet. Originally a very minor warrior, his talents had been recognized, and he had been taken into the Takeda army on the personal recommendation of one of Shingen's veterans, Itagaki Nobutaka, who had been killed at Uedahara in 1548. Yamamoto Kansuke had risen to be Shingen's right-hand man, and was now nearly 70 years old.

It was in his capacity as Shingen's military adviser, the *gun-bugyo*, that he drew up the plans for Operation 'Woodpecker' a somewhat free translation of the term *kitsutsuki no sempo*, which the chronicle *Koyo Gunkan* uses for the scheme that would allow the Takeda to launch a surprise attack on the Uesugi. The woodpecker (*kitsutsuki*) strikes its beak on the bark of a tree, and when the insects rush out through the hole in the bark the bird gobbles them up. That was Yamamoto Kansuke's analogy. It was now early October, and Kosaka Danjo Masanobu, the keeper of Kaizu, was to play the part of the woodpecker.

With a force of 8,000 men he was to climb Saijoyama from the rear by night, and attack

1561
THE FOURTH BATTLE OF KAWANAKAJIMA

Right: Shingen takes a meal before the battle. Every year at Isawa, which is near Kofu, the Battle of Kawanakajima is re-enacted as part of the annual *Shingen-ko* Festival. Here the actor playing Shingen receives a cup of *sake* (rice wine), from one of his *tsukai-ban* (messengers), who are identified by the badge of a busy centipede on their *sashimono*. Shingen's son, Katsuyori, is depicted seated at his right hand.

the Uesugi positions. This would drive the Uesugi army down the north side of the mountain, across the Chikumagawa at the ford of Amenomiya and on to the waiting muzzles and sharp blades of Shingen's main body. Shingen would have left Kaizu at midnight, crossed the river on the far side of Kaizu from Saijoyama, and taken up a prepared battle formation at Hachiman-bara in the centre of the flatlands of Kawan-

akajima, all under the cover of darkness and in total secrecy. As dawn broke, Kenshin's array would be caught between two samurai armies and utterly destroyed.

Operation 'Woodpecker' began, as Yamamoto had planned, at midnight. Takeda Shingen led 8,000 men out of Kaizu, and across the Chikumagawa by the nearest ford to the aptly named Hachimanbara, 'War God Plain', which would have in-

四

1561
THE FOURTH BATTLE OF KAWANAKAJIMA

volved a short march of about two and a half miles. Here, according to the *Koyo Gunkan*, he drew up his army, which covered an area of about 1,500 square yards, in the battle formation known as *kakuyoku*, or 'crane's wing'. The old chronicles are very fond of describing battle formations in such poetic language, giving certain formations names which would be understandable to the samurai clientele for whom these epics were written. A series of set battle formations is implied, and it is more than likely that both Shingen and Kenshin had great skills in arranging these tried and tested formations. The mere fact that the Takeda arrangement was carried out in almost total darkness suggests that hours must have been spent training the Takeda army to move quickly into pre-arranged positions.

51

1561
THE FOURTH BATTLE OF KAWANAKAJIMA

So the Takeda formed their *kakuyoku*, which Yoshihiko Sasama (1968) tells us is the best formation for surrounding an advancing enemy. A screen of arquebusiers and archers protect the vanguard (in this case under the command of Shingen's younger brother, Takeda Nobushige) while the main body of samurai, forming a second and a third division, are spread out behind them like the swept-back wings of a crane. The general's headquarters occupy the centre, protected on both sides by *hatamoto*, the particular chosen samurai, who are 'under the standard', which is the translation of *hatamoto*. A squadron of reserve troops stand on each side, slightly to the rear of the *hatamoto*. There is a rearguard, with more archers and arquebusiers.

Shingen's *maku*, the cloth curtains ornamented with the Takeda *mon*, or badge, were set up to form his headquarters post in the centre of Hachiman Plain, somewhat to the rear of the samurai wings. Here he sat, waiting for the dawn, and hundreds of fleeing Uesugi samurai approaching the *kakuyoku*. However, unknown to Shingen, Uesugi Kenshin had not been idle. His scouts on Saijoyama, or perhaps vigilant spies sent down to Kaizu, reported seeing fires in Kaizu, and signs that Shingen was making a move. Kenshin guessed what the plan might be, and planned a countermove, also to be carried out at dead of night. In total secrecy Uesugi Kenshin descended from Saijoyama by its western flanks. Instead of fleeing before Kosaka's dawn attack the Uesugi army crept carefully down the mountain. To deaden the noise of movement his horses' hooves and bits were padded with cloth, and as Shingen moved to Hachimanbara Kenshin likewise crossed the Chikumagawa, in his case by the ford of Amenomiya, and entered Kawanakajima somewhat to the west of Shingen's position.

We must now ask ourselves, in which direction was the Takeda army facing? A glance at the map shows that it must have been west. To cross by Amenomiya the fleeing Uesugi would have had to swing round to the west, and then presumably would have headed north for the safety of the Zenko-ji and the 'moat' of the Saigawa. The *kakuyoku* would then take them easily in flank. But as dawn broke the Takeda

army peered through the dispersing mist to see the Uesugi army, not fleeing across their front, but bearing down upon them head-on in a fierce charge. The position of the Takeda is confirmed by the fact that Takeda Nobushige in the vanguard received the first assault.

It was a carefully organized attack, which the Uesugi must have practised. As one unit became weary it was replaced by another, a method recorded in the *Koyo Gunkan* as *kuruma gakari*, or 'winding wheel'. Leading the Uesugi vanguard was a certain Kakizaki Izumi-no-kami Kageie, one of the Uesugi Twenty-Eight Generals. His unit of mounted samurai crashed into the Takeda unit commanded by Takeda Nobushige, Shingen's

Left: Takeda Nobushige's division attacks at Kawanakajima. A lively moment from the re-enactment of Kawanakajima at Isawa. The division of Takeda Nobushige, Shingen's younger brother, (identified by the white disc on black of their flags), accompanied by the samurai of Ichijo Nobutatsu, another brother (white and red flag), charge forward against the Uesugi. Nobushige was killed at Kawanakajima, and is buried on the battlefield.

younger brother and his second-in-command. Nobushige died in the fierce hand-to-hand fighting which followed. As Kakizaki's unit withdrew to rest they were replaced by fresh bands of mounted samurai who kept up the pressure. Takemata Hirotsuna led his followers against the veteran Takeda leaders, Naito Masatoyo and Morozumi Bungo-no-kami, and was knocked clean off his horse, the force of the blow as he hit the ground dislodging his helmet. Once again the Uesugi tactic of rotating the front-line troops was put into operation, and Takemata Hirotsuna withdrew to be replaced by another.

As the wheel wound on, Shingen's *gunbugyo*, Yamamoto Kansuke Haruyuki, realized that his carefully made plans had failed. He accepted full responsibility for the disaster which his error of judgement had brought upon them, and resolved to make amends by dying like a true samurai. Taking a long spear he charged alone into the midst of the Uesugi samurai, where he fought fiercely until, overcome by bullet wounds, and wounded in eighty places on his body, he retired to a grassy knoll and committed *hara-kiri*.

Meanwhile, Takeda Shingen, seated on his folding camp-stool, was trying desperately to control his harassed army from his command post. By the good offices of his *tsukai-ban*, or messengers, who were distinguished by the very appropriate device

1561
THE FOURTH BATTLE OF KAWANAKAJIMA

of a busy centipede on their *sashimono* (the banner worn on the back of the armour), full communication was maintained with his officers. Discipline was good, and the *kakuyoku* was holding up well, even though it had not been designed as a defensive formation.

But great danger was at hand. The enemy had by now reached the Takeda headquarters troops, the *hatamoto*, and Shingen's personal bodyguard. Shingen's son, Takeda Yoshinobu, was wounded, and at this point there occurred one of the most famous instances of single combat in samurai history. According to the *Koyo Gunkan* (the only written source for this incident) there came bursting into the curtained enclosure of Takeda Shingen headquarters a single mounted samurai, wearing a white head cowl, and with a green *kataginu* (a form of surcoat) over his armour. It was Uesugi Kenshin himself. He swung his sword at Shingen, who did not have time to draw his own sword, but rose from his camp-stool and parried the blows as best he could with his *gumbai uchiwa*, the heavy war-fan carried by generals, which he had been using for signalling. He received three cuts on his body armour, and took seven on the war-fan until one of his retainers, Hara Osumi-no-kami, came to his aid and attacked the horseman with his spear. The blade glanced off Kenshin's armour, causing the spear shaft to strike the horse's rump, which made the animal rear. By now others of Shingen's guard had rallied to their master's side, and Kenshin was driven off.

The site of this famous skirmish is now called *mitachi nana tachi no ato* ('three sword seven sword place'), and next to it is a fine modern statue depicting the fight between the two generals. Their combat is often depicted in woodblock prints (see page 79 of *The Book of the Samurai* by the present author for a small section from a particularly fine example). Kenshin is usually depicted with sword or spear, his horse knocking to one side the *maku* curtains and wooden shields that surround Shingen.

An alternative tradition has it that it was not Uesugi Kenshin who fought the combat but one of his vanguard, a samurai by the name of Arakawa. Two others of the Twenty-Eight Uesugi Generals, Nakajo

Tokashi and Irobe Katsunaga, the latter officer holding the rank of *gun-bugyo* in the Uesugi army, were also to be later honoured by Kenshin for the part they played in the breakthrough to Shingen's headquarters.

One by one the Takeda samurai fell. After Shingen's brother, and Yamamoto Kansuke, there followed Morozumi Bungo-no-kami, who had suffered the first assault. Also killed was the hero, Hajikano Gengoro, who two years previously had earned great glory during the Takeda assault on the Hojo's Odawara Castle. Yet despite the fierce, rotating attacks by the Uesugi army, the Takeda main body held firm. Obu Saburohei fought back against Kakizaki's samurai. Anayama Nobukie destroyed Shibata of Echigo, and actually succeeded in forcing the Uesugi army back towards

the Chikumagawa, and of course, while this surprise attack was going on the 'woodpecker' force under Kosaka Danjo Masanobu had arrived at the summit of Saijoyama.

Their advance had been conducted in great stealth, and no doubt the silence that greeted them was put down to their skill in failing to attract the attention of Kenshin's sentries. Then they realized what had happened. The Uesugi position was deserted, and they could hear the noise of battle coming from the plain to the north. They immediately descended Saijoyama by the paths leading down to Chikumagawa at the ford of Amenomiya, the same route that they had planned should be the one that a panicking Kenshin would choose. Now the detached Takeda force flew down to the ford to hurry to the aid of Shingen's main body. Uesugi Kenshin had prudently left

the ford of Amenomiya guarded by a detachment of 3,000 men under one of his most reliable generals, Amakasu Omi-no-kami Kagemochi. Here took place possibly the most desperate fighting of the day, with victory going eventually to the Takeda force. When Kosaka and his men forced their way across the ford, the stage was set to reverse all the triumph which had so far been Kenshin's, but would they be in time? The Takeda detached force poured across the river against the rear of the Uesugi samurai, who were now caught between the arms of the pincers, just as the late Yamamoto Kansuke had planned.

Soon the Takeda re-established control. A group of soldiers managed to recover from the Uesugi trophy hunters the heads of Shingen's brother Nobushige and Morozumi Bungo-no-kami, and by midday

1561
THE FOURTH BATTLE OF KAWANAKAJIMA

Left: The single combat at Hachimanbara. The most famous moment during the Fourth Battle of Kawanakajima was the single combat between the two opposing generals, Takeda Shingen and Uesugi Kenshin. This illustration of it is from a painted screen.

Right: Three heroes of the Takeda. Kosaka Danjo Masanobu, Shingen's lover and most trusted general, led the surprise attack on Saijoyama that failed, then converted defeat into victory by forcing the passage of the Chikumagawa against the Uesugi rearguard. Yamagata Masakage (centre) survived Kawanakajima and eventually died in the charge at Nagashino. The figure on the right is Shingen's heir, Katsuyori.

a defeat had been turned into a victory. The Takeda side counted 3,117 enemy heads taken, and Shingen held a triumphant head-viewing ceremony, clutching in his hand, one presumes, the battered war-fan that had saved his life.

On the morning of the following day, a time of truce, Uesugi Kenshin sent three of his generals, Naoe, Amakasu and Usa, to burn what remained of their encampment on Saijoyama. It would appear that Takeda Shingen made no attempt to stop them, nor to interfere with Kenshin's subsequent withdrawal beyond the Saigawa to the Zenko-ji, and, a few days later, back to Echigo province itself. Not that the Takeda army was in much better shape than their opponents. The Uesugi had suffered 72 per cent casualties, and the Takeda, the supposed victors, lost 62 per cent, including several of their most able leaders. That was the Fourth Battle of Kawanakajima, one of the largest encounters in the history of sixteenth-century Japan. There was a fifth battle at Kawanakajima. The two rivals were to fight just one more round before their attentions were drawn to other enemies elsewhere. In September 1564 Shingen advanced on to the Kawanakajima plain and set up camp on a hill called Shiozaki. Kenshin responded and they faced each other once again across the Saigawa. Both armies sat there for sixty days, and after some skirmishing withdrew. This was the Fifth, and final, Battle of Kawanakajima.

Kawanakajima Today

Kawanakajima is one of the most evocative of the sixteenth-century battlefields. The best starting-point is Nagano City. If you have arrived at Nagano from either Tokyo or Nagoya you will have already crossed the battlefield by train. Take a bus (20 minutes) to Matsushiro, and alight at Kawanakajima. The bus-stop is next to Hachimanbara with its splendid statues of the single combat, and the *mitachi nanatachi* monument. There is a simple Shinto shrine among the trees. As well as the site itself there is a modern museum which has a very good audio-visual show, in Japanese, about the Fourth Battle of Kawanakajima. The grave of Morozumi Bungo-no-kami is to the north, on the way back to Nagano. To complete the tour, walk half a mile down to the Chikumagawa River and see Nobushige's grave in the temple called the Tenkyu-ji, which is on the right just before the modern bridge. There is a very interesting little museum, which contains, among other items, one of Shingen's helmets.

Yamamoto Kansuke's grave can be seen by crossing the bridge and heading northwest. Alternatively, take the bus again, or walk, into the pleasant town of Matsushiro and see the ruins of Kaizu Castle, and a number of historic buildings associated with the Sanada family, retainers of the Takeda. The more energetic may then climb Saijoyama (1,600 feet) for the panoramic view from Kenshin's camp.

1570

The Battle of the Anegawa

From the point of view of Oda Nobunaga and Tokugawa Ieyasu, to whose exploits we now return, the most important detail about the cataclysmic Fourth Battle of Kawanakajima was the fact that the Takeda and the Uesugi became so preoccupied with fighting each other that all other clans were neglected, and it was at about the time of the Fourth Battle of Kawanakajima that the alliance between Oda Nobunaga and Tokugawa Ieyasu was finally sealed with no interference from the north.

Nobunaga the Conqueror

During the ten years following Okehazama, Oda Nobunaga grew as a general and a statesman. Now that Ieyasu was allied to him four provinces along the Tokaido were effectively Oda territory. As his victories grew in number his reputation spread to the highest circles in the land, and in 1562 Nobunaga received the honour of a personal letter from the Emperor Ogimachi, who had heard of the great exploits of this obscure young *daimyo*. The letter suggested that the newly rich Nobunaga might care to make some contribution towards the rebuilding of the imperial palace, and also use his newly revealed military skills to help put an end to the many troubles which had long been plaguing the capital.

This request gave Nobunaga the perfect excuse for invading Mino, the province just to the north of Owari. Mino was not on the Tokaido, but lay along the Nakasendo, which soared off into the central mountains, a very important consideration should Nobunaga have to face an attack from the Takeda. Mino was the fief of the Saito family, who ruled the province from their supposedly impregnable fortress of Inabayama (now Gifu). The Saito's recent history had not been a happy one. Saito Dosan Toshimasa (1494–1556) had been a monk (Dosan was his Buddhist name), then returned to the life of a layman as a seller of oil. He had then become a *daimyo* by the process of *gekokujo* ('the high overcome by the low'), the 'high' to him being the previous *daimyo* whom he murdered. He then went to war against Oda Nobuhide, Nobunaga's redoubtable father, who defeated him and forced Dosan to give his daughter in marriage to Nobunaga. Later he turned against his own adopted son, Yoshitatsu, but was defeated by him at the Battle of Nagaragawa in 1556.

At that stage in his career Nobunaga did not dare go to war against Yoshitatsu, who obligingly died in 1561, but the experience of Okehazama, and the approval of the Emperor, gave him the confidence he had lacked in 1556, and in 1564 Nobunaga launched a campaign against Yoshitatsu's son, Tatsuoki.

The taking of the Saito fortress of Inabayama presented any general with a formidable task. It lay on top of a rocky mountain which dominated the plain where the city of Gifu now stands, and was protected to the north by a strong river, the Nagaragawa. Nobunaga entrusted the taking of Inabayama to his up-and-coming young general, Hashiba (later Toyotomi) Hideyoshi. Hideyoshi carried out the task with the efficiency for which he was to become proverbial. Realizing that he needed a secure base from which he could launch attacks, he constructed one at nearby Sunomata, within view of Inabayama. Legend speaks of a castle constructed in the space of one night to impress the Saito. The outerworks, which would have been visible from Inabayama, may well have been built in one night. At any rate it had the desired effect. Inabayama fell, and in 1565 Nobunaga moved his capital there and renamed the place Gifu.

Nobunaga and the Asai

Nobunaga was not the only one who desired Saito Tatsuoki's head. Asai Nagamasa (1545–73) also had considerable interests in this part of Japan. He held lands in Omi province, which is the province the Nakasendo entered on leaving Mino, *en*

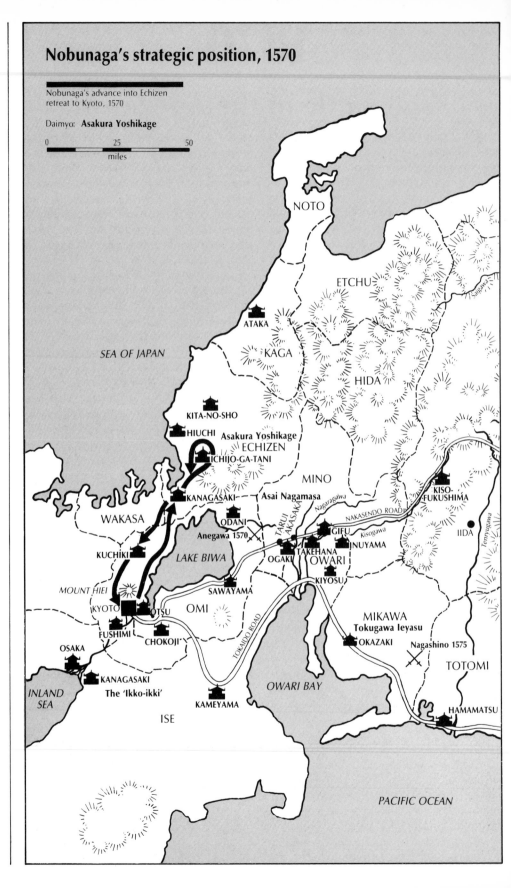

Nobunaga's strategic position, 1570

Nobunaga's advance into Echizen
retreat to Kyoto, 1570

Daimyo: **Asakura Yoshikage**

0   25   50
miles

NOTO

ETCHU

ATAKA

KAGA

HIDA

SEA OF JAPAN

KITA-NO-SHO

HIUCHI   Asakura Yoshikage
          ECHIZEN
ICHIJO-GA-TANI

MINO

KISO-
FUKUSHIMA

KANAGASAKI   Asai Nagamasa

WAKASA   ODANI
          Anegawa 1570   TARUI   Nagaragawa   NAKASENDO ROAD
                          AKASAKA   IIDA
KUCHIKI   OGAKI   GIFU   Kisogawa
          LAKE BIWA   TAKEHANA INUYAMA
                                 OWARI
MOUNT HIEI   KIYOSU
KYOTO   OTSU   OMI
FUSHIMI   SAWAYAMA   MIKAWA
                            Tokugawa Ieyasu
OSAKA   CHOKOJI   OKAZAKI   Nagashino 1575
KANAGASAKI   TOTOMI
The 'Ikko-ikki'   TOKAIDO ROAD
INLAND   OWARI BAY
SEA   KAMEYAMA
                                        HAMAMATSU
ISE

PACIFIC OCEAN

五

1570
THE BATTLE OF
THE ANEGAWA

route for Kyoto. Much of Omi province was water (the famous Lake Biwa, which divides Japan in two), and the chief castle of the Asai was Odani, east of the lake and north of the Nakasendo, a fairly typical *yama-shiro*, built on a wooded hill in the style of the times.

Asai Nagamasa had already been to war against Saito Tatsuoki and had besieged him in the Saito's local stronghold, the castle of Ogaki, on the Nakasendo, when Nobunaga came on the scene in 1564. Nagamasa was expecting to seize half of the Saito domains when Nobunaga opposed him. It was the beginning of a long conflict

between the houses of Asai and Oda, of which the great Battle of the Anegawa in 1570 was its most furious expression.

The first few years of their opposition were concluded peacefully by Nobunaga marrying his sister to Asai Nagamasa. Her name was O-ichi, and she was regarded as being a very great beauty. At about the same time Nobunaga married his adopted daughter to Takeda Katsuyori, son of the great Shingen. Both of these moves, which seemed so benevolent and innocent, were calculated acts of strategy. Both served to protect his northern and western flanks from attack as Nobunaga quietly, and very

1570
THE BATTLE OF THE ANEGAWA

Left: Asai Nagamasa. Asai Nagamasa (1545–73) was married to Oda Nobunaga's sister, but this did not prevent them from continuing a long war.

五

1570
THE BATTLE OF
THE ANEGAWA

successfully, began to put into operation the dream that had eluded Imagawa Yoshimoto. In 1560 Nobunaga had prevented Imagawa Yoshimoto from moving on Kyoto. In 1568 Nobunaga did it himself. He marched his army into the capital, accompanied by a young man whose very existence, and whose desperate pleas for help, had provided Nobunaga with the legitimacy to rule. This young man was to become the fifteenth, and, as it was to prove, the last Ashikaga shogun: Yoshiaki. He had escaped when assassins had murdered the thirteenth Ashikaga Shogun, and set up as their puppet the fourteenth of the line. Now the legitimate shogun was restored to his place by the greatest *daimyo* in the land.

The Retreat from Echizen

Nobunaga's occupation of Kyoto in 1568 meant that henceforth he would have the difficult task of holding the line from Gifu to the capital. The eastern side of Lake Biwa looked fairly safe: his brother-in-law, Asai Nagamasa, ruled from there, but north of Kyoto, up the western shores of Lake Biwa, lay Echizen province, the territory of the Asakura, a well-respected clan ruled by Asakura Yoshikage (1533–73). In 1562 Yoshikage had defeated an army of the Ikko-ikki, the fanatical Buddhist sect, which was no mean feat in itself, and was one of the *daimyo* who had been approached by Ashikaga Yoshiaki prior to Nobunaga's accepting the challenge of the rightful shogun. Yoshikage had declined to help him, and seeing what Nobunaga had made of Yoshiaki, Toshikage must have regretted the missed opportunity. When the new shogun summoned him to Kyoto in 1570 it was salt rubbed into the wound. He refused to go, thinking, quite rightly, that it was Nobunaga's doing, and a way of showing his superiority over him. Infuriated by Asakura's resolve, Nobunaga set off to teach him a lesson by raiding his provinces. His army left Kyoto and headed up the western side of Lake Biwa under the shadow of Mount Hiei.

His first objective was the fortress of Kanagasaki (now the city of Tsuruga), whose taking he entrusted to Hideyoshi. The spirited fight for the gate is illustrated opposite. He then pressed on for Asakura's main base of Ichijo-ga-tani, which lay

farther into Echizen, and was making plans for a siege when he heard some alarming news: his brother-in-law, Asai Nagamasa, had joined Asakura Yoshikage in an alliance against him. The Asai had left Odani and were heading rapidly towards the northern tip of Lake Biwa. The danger was clear. Nobunaga's entire army could be cut off from both Kyoto and Gifu, and attacked from two sides. His generals urged a rapid retreat before Asai Nagamasa's army arrived. Toyotomi Hideyoshi and Tokugawa Ieyasu volunteered for the unglamorous part of providing the rearguard action, and Nobunaga's army began to retrace their steps as far as the border with Omi province, and then swung to the west, and took by-roads via Kuchiki back to Kyoto and safety.

The Battle of the Anegawa

As soon as Nobunaga was able to reorganize and re-equip his army he took the offensive against his treacherous brother-in-law, Asai Nagamasa. His objective was Nagamasa's castle of Odani, and his strategy was straightforward. He left Kyoto by the Nakasendo, and turned off this main road to the north, beside Lake Biwa, somewhere near present-day Maibara. The first river he came to was the Anegawa, which flows from east to west and enters Lake Biwa just north of Nagahama. Nobunaga arrived here on 21 July 1570. Somewhat to the south of this river Asai Nagamasa had another fortress – Yokoyama, a *yamashiro* like Odani to the north. Oda Nobunaga detached a siege force against Yokoyama, and drew up the remainder of his army on

五

1570
THE BATTLE OF THE ANEGAWA

Left: Asakura Yoshikage. Asakura Yoshikage (1533–73) was the ally of Asai Nagamasa against Oda Nobunaga, and shared with him in the defeat of the Anegawa.

Left: The attack on Kanagasaki Castle. The war between Oda Nobunaga and the families of Asai and Asakura, of which the Battle of the Anegawa is the best-known contest, lasted for many years. The taking of the fortress of Kanagasaki (now called Tsuruga) in 1570 was the beginning of the campaign that led to the Battle of the Anegawa. In this illustration from the 1860 edition of the *Ehon Taiko-ki* the brave warriors are identified for the reader by emblazoning their names on their *sashimono* flags.

五

1570
THE BATTLE OF
THE ANEGAWA

the southern bank of the Anegawa, where he rested and waited for Ieyasu to join him with reinforcements from Mikawa province. Asai, unsurprisingly, asked for help from Asakura Yoshikage.

Ieyasu brought 5,000 men to join Nobunaga's 23,000, against whom the allied Asai and Asakura armies numbered about 10,000 each. Nobunaga therefore had the advantage of numbers, but some of his troops were of doubtful reliability, because they had been levied for service from lands owned by Nobunaga in Omi province, which had previously belonged to the Asai. The ever-reliable Toyotomi Hideyoshi was put in charge of this questionable contingent.

Further questions were asked when Nobunaga changed his dispositions the night before the battle. He had originally intended that the Tokugawa troops, and the samurai of Inaba Ittetsu, should attack Asai, but Nobunaga had a very personal grudge against this gentleman, and resolved to oppose Asai himself. He arranged his army thirteen ranks deep to absorb the impact of a charge. The layout is shown in the map on page 62. Ieyasu was on the left flank, facing the Asakura.

It was the middle of the summer, and already light when the battle began at 4 a.m. As the day wore on the sun, climbing higher into the sky, blazed down on the two armies. At first it was almost as though there were two separate battles being fought: the Tokugawa against the Asakura,

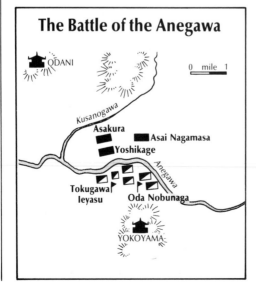

The Battle of the Anegawa

and the Oda upstream against the Asai. Both sides waded into the river, which was sluggish and about three feet deep, and fought furiously, the sweat pouring off them and mingling with the waters of the river which soon were stained with red.

On the Tokugawa side the fight ebbed and flowed across and within the waters of the Anegawa. Ieyasu was in the thick of the fighting, and was attacked by an enemy samurai who had mingled with his *hatamoto*. Then, in one of those bold strokes of which he was master, Ieyasu sent his second division under Honda Tadakatsu and Sakakibara Yasumasa on to Asakura's flank. In an incident similar to the famous single combat at Kawanakajima, a certain samurai called Sasai Masayasu, armed only

Left: The Anegawa. The wide river bed of the Anegawa, photographed in May 1986, looking across towards the site of the Oda positions.

with a spear, fought his way to Asakura's headquarters, only to be blasted by a fusillade of arquebus fire.

At this point we read of another splendid exploit of samurai heroism, and from the opposite side. The battles of sixteenth-century Japan, though characterized by the movement of considerable numbers of troops and a growing use of strategy, still found room for the cherished notion of the brave individual samurai gaining heads for his lord and glory for himself, and Anegawa is no exception. Honda Tadakatsu had launched his flank attack, which was so successful that Asakura Kagetake, the commander-in-chief of Yoshikage's army at the Anegawa, was completely surrounded in the furious mêlée. It was essential that the

Asakura army withdraw to the northern bank, and a certain samurai called Makara Jurozaemon Naotaka, a retainer of the Asakura, volunteered to cover their retreat. 'I am a person called Makara Jurozaemon,' he shouted in a loud voice. 'If anyone forgets it I shall show who I am by gaining my customary victory!'

This Makara Jurozaemon was apparently a giant of a man, who carried a *no-dachi* sword with a blade more than five feet long, which he called his *tairo-tachi* ('the eldest sword'). A *no-dachi* was normally swung with two hands, rather like the Scottish claymore, but Makara Jurozaemon held his in one hand, and swung it from the saddle! Like the samurai of old, whose stories he would have been told as a child, Makara

63

Right: Anegawa from Odani. The river Anegawa can be seen in the middle distance looking from the summit of Odani, the site of Asai Nagamasa's castle. The rectangular areas are ricefields.

bellowed out a challenge to anyone from the Tokugawa side who would come to fight him. This was a good diversionary tactic to adopt at any time in samurai history (Kurikara is another example where it is done by the entire army), and Makara was not disappointed. His challenge was first accepted by a vassal of the Tokugawa called Ogasawara Nagatada, whom Makara killed.

He was then joined by his eldest son, Makara Jurosaburo Naomoto, and together father and son faced repeated attacks by Tokugawa samurai, Naotaka armed with his *tairo-tachi*, his son with a shorter weapon which he called his *jirotachi* ('second oldest sword'). Gradually the Asakura army managed to disengage itself and pull back across the river, as the two Makaras followed slowly, swinging their huge weapons in wide circles and lopping off limbs.

Their downfall came at the hands of four men of Mikawa province, three of whom were brothers: Kosaka Shikibu, Kosaka Gorojiro, Kosaka Rokurogoro and Yamada Muneroku, who attacked the Makaras together. Makara Jurozaemon Naotaka met the first named with force, and swung his enormous sword at him, which cut Kosaka Shikibu on the thigh, then with a second slash knocked the helmet off his head,

smashing it to the ground. He then cut through Shikibu's spear. At this Shikibu's younger brother, Kosaka Gorojiro, ran to his assistance, and was met by a vicious sweep to his side. Yamada Muneroku, a veteran warrior, 60 years old, lost his weapon when his spear shaft parted under a blow from Makara, leaving the third brother, Rokurogoro, to join in the fray. He was armed with a cross-bladed spear, and managed to hook one of the cross-blades under Makara's armour and haul him from his horse to the ground. Makara got up, and shouted 'Whoever takes my head will earn great glory!' a speech which ended abruptly when a sword was swung at his neck.

So in spite of one left arm and one right arm being cut off (exactly to whom they belonged is not clear!), the four Mikawa samurai managed to defeat the giant and take his head. His son, Makara Jurosaburo Naomoto, seeing his father defeated, tried to withdraw to the Asakura army while attempting to avenge his father, but was met by a samurai who introduced himself as Aoki Jozaemon, and engaged him in fierce fighting, at the end of which the younger Makara was killed. 'The colour faded from the cheeks of the Asakura as their two

Far left: The site of the Battle of the Anegawa. The battle site of the Anegawa is marked by this memorial beside the Anegawa, where the Asai/Asakura faction made camp.

Left: The 'headstone' of Odani. The ruins of Odani Castle, which have recently been excavated, reveal many interesting features about samurai life in the 'mountain castles' of the Sengoku Period. This boulder, half-way up the path, was used for displaying the severed heads of the enemy, as illustrated by the author(!).

heroes fell,' writes Mitsueda (1977), but their sacrifice had not been in vain, because their rearguard action had allowed the army to rally, even though they were then pursued for a considerable distance.

That put paid to the Asakura, but further upstream the Asai had reversed the positions. A samurai of the Asai called Endo Kizaemon had resolved to take Nobunaga's head, and was only cut down, by a samurai called Takenaka Kyusaku, when he was quite close to his target. It is surprising to read that Nobunaga was not wearing armour, only a light summer *kimono* under a black *haori*, and a lightweight helmet called a *jingasa*. Seeing Nobunaga's army in dire straits the Tokugawa attacked Asai's right flank, and Inaba Ittetsu, who until then had been held in reserve, fell on his left. Even the besiegers of Yokoyama Castle left their lines to join in. The result was a victory for Oda Nobunaga, who showed his gratitude to Ieyasu by presenting him with a sword, and an arrowhead that had once belonged to the legendary Minamoto Tametomo.

Anegawa was indecisive, in that it did not mean the immediate end of the Asai and the Asakura. Over the next three years Nobunaga wore them down, and in 1573 he returned to the Anegawa, or rather crossed it and laid siege to Odani. This time there was no Asakura clan to relieve it. Ichijo-gatani had already fallen. Seeing that all was lost Asai Nagamasa entrusted his wife and her three daughters to her brother, Oda Nobunaga, and committed *hara-kiri* as the forest and the castle blazed around him. There was a pathetic scene when the survivors' procession halted a little way from Odani, and O-ichi and the little girls descended from their palanquins to witness the burning mountain where Asai Nagamasa was committing suicide. After paying their last respects they re-entered their carriages to be taken to Kyoto.

Anegawa Today
The nearest town to the Anegawa is Nagahama. A taxi, or a friend with a car, is essential if you wish to visit this site, which is rather disappointing compared to other battlefields. There is a monument on the northern bank where the Asai and the Asakura made camp, but little else. The river is probably little changed from 1570. The recently excavated ruins of Odani, and the grave of Asai Nagamasa, are a short distance away, and are well worth a detour if you have transport.

五

1570
THE BATTLE OF
THE ANEGAWA

Right: The grave of Asai Nagamasa. Asai Nagamasa's grave lies at the top of the hill on which was built the castle of Odani.

1572

The Battle of Mikata-ga-Hara

The Battle of Mikata-ga-Hara is one of the most interesting conflicts of Medieval Japan. It pitted the old and mighty Takeda Shingen against the young Tokugawa Ieyasu in a furious pitched battle, which was only saved from being a complete defeat of the Tokugawa by a classic rear-guard action.

Hamamatsu

Mikata-ga-Hara lies to the north of the town of Hamamatsu, which is a few miles from the sea almost in the centre of Japan, beside a large and beautiful lake called Hama-no-ko. Few towns, in an archipelago as complicated as the Japanese islands, could claim to be the actual centre of anywhere, but Hamamatsu has for centuries had this particular claim to fame: that it lies exactly midway along the famous Tokaido, the Eastern Sea Road from Kyoto to Edo, which was the main artery of pre-modern Japan.

In a previous chapter we looked at the Tokaido in the context of the Battle of Okehazama. Traditionally its length is measured from the Nihonbashi ('the Japan bridge') in Edo, to the centre of Kyoto. Edo, which is now the city of Tokyo, entered history with the defeat of the Hojo clan at Odawara in 1592. Tokugawa Ieyasu, the future shogun, was given the Hojo territories as a reward, and chose Edo as his base. Twenty years before this event, at the time of the Battle of Mikata-ga-Hara, Edo was largely unregarded, being a minor castle of the Hojo and a good fishing village. As a result, although the line of the Tokaido was well recognized and much used, it lacked what was to become one of its traditional ends, so that the important staging-post of Hamamatsu was not in any sense half-way to anywhere. None the less, it had considerable military significance in 1572, because it was then Tokugawa Ieyasu's capital, and as such became the site of one of the fiercest battles of Medieval Japan, which in its own ironic way

nearly settled the fate of the future city of Tokyo by wiping the Tokugawa family from the map of Japan.

This battle is not called the Battle of Hamamatsu, even though the fighting extended to the very gates of Hamamatsu Castle. It takes its name from the plateau a few miles to the north called Mikata-ga-Hara, the high ground from where the attack on the Tokugawa was launched. Hamamatsu's position on the map suggests its importance. Ieyasu had moved there in 1570, thereby extending the influence of his ally, Oda Nobunaga, that much further along the Tokaido. It was in a highly strategic place, lying almost at the mouth of the Tenryugawa, the river that drains the mountains of Kai and Shinano – territory of the mighty Takeda Shingen.

By 1572 Shingen was at the height of his powers. The backbone of his army was still his mounted samurai, under the command of his Twenty-Four Generals, though time had wrought some changes in their ranks since Kawanakajima. The great change brought about in Shingen himself was in the new breadth of vision which the past ten years had given him. Uesugi Kenshin was less of a threat to him, and they had fought their fifth, and final Battle of Kawanakajima in 1564, but Shingen now realized that his greatest enemy lay to the west in the person of Oda Nobunaga.

Nobunaga the Destroyer

Nobunaga possessed the centre. He had won the victory of Anegawa, and gone on from that to carry out his infamous raid on the monks of Mount Hiei in 1571. This was probably the only military action of Nobunaga's career so controversial that even some of his own generals had opposed the move, but it had gone ahead none the less. Nobunaga had done it for sound military reasons. The Asai and the Asakura were as yet undefeated. When marching to Echizen in 1570 he had passed beneath the vast bulk of Mount Hiei, and

六

1572
THE BATTLE OF
MIKATA-GA-HARA

Right: Takeda Shingen. A portrait of the renowned Shingen, taken from a *kakemono* in the Preservation Hall of Nagashino Castle.

realized how it threatened his lines of communication to the north from Kyoto. The holy mountain, which lay in the 'Demon Gate' quarter, according to Chinese geomancy, and therefore protected the capital from evil, had been revered for centuries. It was the centre of Tendai Buddhism, but during earlier centuries had visited its own wrath upon Kyoto in the form of armies of warrior monks. In Nobunaga's day the warrior monks had allied themselves with the fanatical Ikko-sect confederates against him. Mount Hiei was an easy target. The mountain was surrounded by a huge army, and Nobunaga's troops simply advanced up the paths and shot or hacked to death every living thing they met, as a warning to any armies, clerical or lay, that dared oppose him.

The destruction of Mount Hiei gave any *daimyo* a perfect religious excuse for making war on Nobunaga, and as Shingen was a Buddhist monk he must have been no exception. It is quite clear that Shingen saw that an eventual conflict with Nobunaga was his destiny, and that Shingen expected it to be a cataclysmic event whereby he would supplant Nobunaga as warlord of

Kyoto. He had the leisure to plan his moves, and to safeguard them in the time-honoured fashion of marriage alliances, the giving of hostages, and guarantees of support. Shingen wove a complex web. He was married to the sister of the wife of the Chief Priest of the Ikko sect of Buddhism, and through this connection hoped to use the Ikko-*ikki* ('Ikko leagues') of the provinces of Echizen, Kaga and the Noto peninsula to harass Uesugi Kenshin.

Shingen had also reached a new understanding with his son-in-law, Hojo Ujimasa, with whom he had been at war for years, which safeguarded his eastern flank, but in case the Hojo proved treacherous he made a further secret alliance with the families of Satomi and Satake so that they could descend on his rear. One result of the new Takeda/Hojo alliance was that Imagawa Ujizane, the son of the late Imagawa Yoshi-moto, was banished from the Hojo domain, and went to seek refuge with the man who had abandoned him after Okehazama – Oda Nobunaga's ally, Tokugawa Ieyasu.

Tokugawa Ieyasu was not Shingen's greatest threat, merely his most immediate challenge now that he had moved his head-

1572
THE BATTLE OF MIKATA-GA-HARA

Left: Tokugawa Ieyasu. Tokugawa Ieyasu fought the Battle of Mikata-ga-Hara at the age of 29. This modern statue of him his in the grounds of Okazaki Castle, where he was born.

六

1572
THE BATTLE OF
MIKATA-GA-HARA

Right: Hamamatsu Castle. Hamamatsu Castle, on the Tokaido, was Ieyasu's headquarters, and Shingen's immediate objective in the campaign that led to the Battle of Mikata-ga-Hara. The present keep is a modern reconstruction.

quarters from Okazaki to Hamamatsu, an act which Takeda Shingen regarded as provocative. Both Nobunaga and Shingen had much to gain by maintaining a semblance of cordial relations between them, and Shingen's policy was a straightforward one of keeping peace with Nobunaga until he had destroyed his ally Ieyasu. Nobunaga, meanwhile, was actively courting Uesugi Kenshin, hoping thereby to neutralize any rising by the Ikko-ikki. Nobunaga advised Ieyasu to withdraw to Okazaki and avoid any conflict with Shingen while the building of alliances went on, but Ieyasu would have none of it. He was 29 years old and an experienced leader of samurai. Retreat, any retreat, was out of the question. So Ieyasu remained in Hamamatsu, and Takeda Shingen made the first move against him. He marched his army out of his capital of Fuchu (the present-day city of Kofu) in October 1572, relying on the coming snows, rather than the Ikko-ikki, to keep Uesugi Kenshin off his tail.

The Advance to Mikawa

Takeda Shingen's route is an interesting one. (See the map on page 73.) He did not

take the most straightforward way, which would have been to head due south from Kofu, skirt Mount Fuji to the west, join the Tokaido near the present-day town of Fujinomiya, and approach Hamamatsu from the east. This would have placed him under the potential danger of an attack by the Hojo. Instead he first headed north, then swung across the northern foothills of the Southern Japan Alps by the mountain pass that leads through Takato. From Takato he dropped down into the valley of the Tenryugawa and passed through Iida, thus approaching Ieyasu from the north without leaving his own territory. His first objective in Tokugawa lands was the castle of Futamata.

The *Koyo Gunkan* gives the total strength of the Takeda army as 35,000 men, including several thousand from the Hojo, though this figure also includes 5,000 under his celebrated general, Yamagata Masakage, who provided a diversion to Shingen's main thrust by attacking eastern Mikawa. His troops probably marched with the rest of the Takeda army as far as Sakuma, where they turned towards the south-west, following the valley through which now runs the

六

1572
THE BATTLE OF
MIKATA-GA-HARA

Right: The Battle of Mikata-ga-Hara. This *ukiyoe* print depicts a tense moment during the battle when Naito Masatoyo charged into the Tokugawa ranks.

Right: Oyamada Nobushige. Oyamada Nobushige, one of the Takeda 'Twenty-Four Generals', served with great distinction in the Takeda vanguard at Mikata-ga-Hara.

Iida line of the Japanese Railway. It is interesting to note that this route must have passed Nagashino Castle, where Yamagata was destined to lose his life three years later. But in 1572 there were no hindrances to their advance, and Yamagata's samurai captured the strategically important Yoshida Castle on the Tokaido, the ruins of which are to be found in the present-day Toyohashi City. This was an important gain for Shingen, because it cut Tokugawa Ieyasu off from any support from the west. His victorious contingent then turned east (Sadler incorrectly makes them turn west) to join Shingen's main body, which had by now taken Futamata Castle to the north of Hamamatsu.

Ieyasu was therefore in extreme peril. He had been joined in Hamamatsu by reinforcements sent by Nobunaga under the generals Sakuma Nobumori, Hiraide Norihide and Takigawa Kazumasa, who, one presumes, must have arrived before Yamagata's taking of Yoshida. None was in favour of attacking Shingen. They reasoned that Shingen's objective was not Ieyasu, but Nobunaga himself, and that Hamamatsu should prepare for a siege. If Shingen's army moved on, leaving a masking force, perhaps the siege could be broken and Shingen taken in the rear. But Ieyasu was determined to stop Shingen by battle rather than a siege.

The Takeda army was drawn up on the high ground of Mikata-ga-Hara. The *Koyo Gunkan*, with its love of order, gives Shingen's formation as *gyorin*, the fish-scale formation, one of the classic battle formations which supposedly entices an enemy to attack. According to Sasama (1963) *gyorin* is similar in appearance to the *kakuyoku* formation Shingen used at Kawanakajima, but is much narrower across its frontage. The vanguard samurai are spread out with the second divisions holding the flanks.

If forcing an attack were the intention, it succeeded admirably, and Ieyasu led his army out to oppose Shingen, though he was outnumbered by about three to one. The *Koyo Gunkan* gives Ieyasu's total as 11,000, of which 8,000 were his own troops, and 3,000 the reinforcements from Nobunaga. These he drew up in a line (a variant of *kakuyoku*, according to the *Koyo Gunkan*),

1572
THE BATTLE OF MIKATA-GA-HARA

The Battle of Mikata-ga-Hara

Takeda
Shinken

Tokugawa
Ieyasu

SAIGADOKE

Magomegawa

0   mile   1

HAMAMATSU

with his own headquarters troops a little to the rear. On his left flank were three fine Mikawa generals, Matsudaira Ietada, Honda Tadakatsu and Ishikawa Kazumasa, with Ogasawara Nagayoshi, whose family was originally from Shinano. Shingen had taken these lands from them, so they had a great enmity against the Takeda. On his right flank, leading down to the Mago-megawa, he placed the three Oda contingents, with the trustworthy Mikawa general, Saka Tadatsugu, on the extreme flank.

Shingen's 'fish-scales' were fronted by six of his Twenty-Four Generals. Oyamada Nobushige led the vanguard. Naito Masa-toyo and Yamagata Masakage formed a second rank. Shingen's son, Katsuyori, and Obata Masamori were the third, with Baba Nobuharu the fourth. Shingen's main body of about 15,000 lay behind them. The sight of such a host at close hand encouraged Ieyasu's commanders to attempt further to persuade him to withdraw, and, as Torii Motohiro advised him, let them march past into Mikawa and conveniently fall upon their rear at a later stage. Once again Ieyasu turned down the suggestion, and at about four o'clock in the afternoon, as snow was beginning to fall, the front ranks of the Tokugawa opened fire on the Takeda samurai.

The Takeda forward troops attacked them with great vigour, as shown in the nine-teenth-century *ukiyo-e* print on page 72, which depicts Naito Masatoyo, wearing a white horsehair plume on his helmet,

assaulting the division of Honda Tadakatsu, whose well-known stag-antlers helmet is seen on the right. Honda and the other Mikawa men withstood the assault well, but the three commanders sent by Nobunaga had not the same spirit for a desperate fight. Takigawa and Sakuma withdrew immediately. Hiraide Norihide stood firm until he was killed and his division overrun, leaving Sakai Tadatsugu isolated on the wing. At this point Shingen calmly withdrew his forward units to rest and sent in the fresh troops under Obata and Takeda Katsuyori, much as Kenshin had done against him at Kawanakajima. Saigusa Moritomo, another of Shingen's Twenty-Four Generals, led fifty horsemen in a fierce assault. It was getting dark, and seeing the

Tokugawa troops reeling Shingen ordered a general assault by the main body.

The Fighting Retreat

Very soon the Tokugawa army was in full retreat. Ieyasu sent Okubo Tadayo back to Saigadake, where the ground began to drop away down to Hamamatsu, there to plant Ieyasu's personal golden fan standard as a rallying-point for the troops. Ieyasu himself was still in a fighting mood, and was all for charging back into the Takeda ranks to assist his comrade, Mizuno Masashige, who was surrounded, or to die in the attempt. By now the Takeda had reached Ieyasu's headquarters troops and were surrounding his bodyguard *hatamoto*, when the keeper of Hamamatsu Castle, Natsume

75

1572
THE BATTLE OF
MIKATA-GA-HARA

Right: The gorge of Saigadake. During the night of the Battle of Mikata-ga-Hara the Tokugawa troops, who were familiar with the locality, enticed the Takeda into this gorge, which forms a natural ravine at the southern end of the Mikata-ga-Hara plateau.

Jirozaemon Yoshinobu, who was 55 years old, rode out from the fortress to persuade his lord to withdraw, offering to hold back the enemy while he did so.

Yoshinobu pleaded with Ieyasu to consider the future of his family, and for their sake not risk losing his life. With the authority granted to him solely by his age, he tugged on Ieyasu's bridle to bring his horse around, and struck it on the rump with his spear shaft, calling out to Ieyasu's attendants to ride with their lord for the

castle. Yoshinobu turned back to the Takeda shouting 'I am Ieyasu!' and plunged into the fight to be killed. Whether or not his words could be heard above the din of battle, his courageous attempt at substitution allowed Ieyasu to escape, and Yoshinobu is now the only samurai of either side to have a personal memorial on the site of the battle.

But the fight was by no means over for Ieyasu. Naruse Masayoshi, Toyama Kosaku and Endo Ukon were only three of the samurai who sacrificed themselves for their master during the desperate retreat; their graves lie at Mikata-ga-Hara. Amano Yasukage, who survived the action, kicked the bow out of a Takeda soldier's hands as he took aim at Ieyasu, so the withdrawal must have been a closely fought action. Ieyasu himself put an arrow through one Takeda man who ran at him with a spear.

Hamamatsu Castle had of course now lost its commander, Natsume Yoshinobu, and the noise from the north must have made its soldiers certain that they had lost their lord as well. To put heart into the defenders Ieyasu had earlier sent to the castle a samurai who had cut the head from a warrior wearing a monk's cowl, which he proclaimed as the head of Shingen, but it had given them only a temporary respite from worry, and the rapid arrival of Ieyasu with apparently only five men left made it seem that defeat was certain. Torii Moto-tada was just giving orders for the gates to be shut and barred when Ieyasu inter-rupted him. To shut the gates was precisely what Takeda Shingen expected them to do, he reasoned. Instead he ordered the gates to be left open for their retreating com-rades, and a huge brazier to be lit to guide them home. To add to the confident air Sakai Tadatsugu took a large war drum and beat it in the tower beside the gate. His lord, apparently well satisfied with the pre-cautions they had taken, took a meal of three bowls of rice and went to sleep. The *Mikawa Fudo-ki* adds that his snores re-sounded through the room.

As Ieyasu had predicted, when Yamagata Masakage and Baba Nobuharu, who led the Takeda advance to the castle, saw the open gates and the light and heard the drum, they immediately suspected a trick. The *Mikawa Fudo-ki* has them comment upon the Tokugawa dead, that all who had died in the advance lay face downwards, while those killed in the retreat lay on their backs. None had turned his back to the enemy. The Mikawa *bushi* were men to be reckoned with.

The Battle of Saigadake
So no night-time assault was made on the castle, and the Takeda army camped for the night on the battlefield near Saigadake. The weather conditions indicated that it would

be an uncomfortable stay, so the Tokugawa men resolved to make it as unpleasant as possible, thereby keeping up the fiction of a strongly defended castle. It was an area the Tokugawa men knew well, so Okubo Tadayo and Amano Yasukage gathered a volunteer force of sixteen arquebusiers and 100 other footsoldiers and attacked the Takeda encampment at Saigadake. Here the plain of Mikata-ga-Hara is split by a narrow canyon, which the modern road crosses at Saigadake next to the battle monument. The Tokugawa troops led the Takeda back to this ravine, which is about one mile long, fifty yards wide, and 100 feet deep in places. It still provides a surprise for the visitor, though most of the area is now built on, and it provided a greater surprise for the confused Takeda soldiers.

Okubo is further credited with building a dummy bridge, covered with cloth, across the gap, which seems unlikely as the whole action was fought during one night, though the area round here is still called Nuno no hashi, or 'Cloth Bridge'. Bridge or not, many scores of Takeda samurai and horses fell into this ravine, where the Tokugawa troops fired on them and cut them up as they lay helpless. After the battle, according to legend, local people were troubled by the moans from the ghosts coming from this valley, so in 1574 Ieyasu established a temple at Saigadake called the Soen-do, where a monk called Soen prayed for the repose of the souls.

Thus did Ieyasu show himself to be as much a master of psychological warfare as he was a field commander of repute. Shingen held a council of war, and impres-sed by the tenacity of the Tokugawa, re-solved to withdraw to his mountains and return the following year, rather than risk a winter siege of Hamamatsu, which an all-out assault might well have taken. So the whole Takeda army pulled back, fooled completely by the Tokugawa.

As to Shingen's relations with Nobunaga, the head of Hiraide Norihide was ample proof of Nobunaga's determination to oppose him either directly or through others. The time for pretence had passed, so Shingen sent it with an appropriate letter to Nobunaga, denouncing him for breaking off their entirely illusory peaceful co-existence. Now that the enmity was out in

1572
THE BATTLE OF MIKATA-GA-HARA

1572
THE BATTLE OF
MIKATA-GA-HARA

Right: The Soen-do. Local people were dismayed by the groans coming from the ghosts of samurai killed during the Saigadake battle. Ieyasu therefore caused this temple to be raised, and installed a priest, called Soen, to pray for the repose of their souls.

the open Takeda Shingen renewed his attempts to destroy Ieyasu, and when the snows melted he returned in early 1573 to lay siege to Ieyasu's castle of Noda, in Mikawa province. According to an enduring legend the defenders, knowing their end was near, decided to dispose of their stocks of *sake* (rice wine), in the most appropriate manner. The noises of their celebrations could be heard by the besieging camp, who also took note of one garrison where a samurai was playing a flute. Takeda Shingen approached the ramparts to listen and a vigilant guard, less drunk than his companions, took an arquebus and put a bullet through his head. The death of Shingen was kept secret for as long as the Takeda could manage. Their attempts at deception, and the huge responsibility inherited by Shingen's son, Katsuyori, are the theme of Kurosawa's great film *Kagemusha*. It was the beginning of a long process of rebuilding for the Takeda family, which was eventually to be resolved on the field of Nagashino.

Mikata-ga-Hara Today
Hamamatsu can be reached easily by train from either Tokyo or Osaka. Take the J. N. R. Tokaido Line train to Hamamatsu, which is served by the *Shinkansen*, the famous bullet train. The bus station is

across the road from the railway station in the city square. As much of Mikata-ga-Hara is now built over, Saigadake is the best area to visit. Take a bus heading for Saigadake, and alight at the bus-stop next to the tall memorial to Natsume Motoyoshi. A few yards further on the road crosses the ravine of Saigadake by means of the modern 'Cloth Bridge'. There is a bamboo grove at the bottom of the ravine. On the far side of the ravine is the battle monument, and the compound of the Soen-do, which is also a public garden. Those interested can continue north to Mikata-ga-Hara itself in the footsteps of Ieyasu's troops, where empty fields give some impression of the old battlefield.

Hamamatsu Castle is well worth a visit, and is a short bus ride from the station. In the grounds is a statue of Tokugawa Ieyasu. The keep is a modern reconstruction, but very well done, and houses a small museum with some interesting armour and weapons. From its upper storey there is a good view of Mikata-ga-Hara to the north, showing how close the Takeda came to destroying Ieyasu's capital.

An additional excursion can be made to the Mitsuke Tenjin Shrine, east of Hamamatsu across the Tenryugawa, where Sakai Tadatsugu's famous drum is preserved.

1575

The Battle of Nagashino

Left: Takeda Katsuyori. Takeda Katsuyori, son of Shingen, leads the Takeda cavalry into action at the Battle of Nagashino. Katsuyori is identified by the character 'dai' on his flag. This is from a modern copy of the famous painted screen of Nagashino.

The Battle of Nagashino holds a special place in samurai history. In purely military terms, if Nagashino had been Oda Nobunaga's only victory his reputation would have been secured. Instead it is the culmination of a brilliant military career, and a milestone in Japanese history. But Nagashino has an additional, personal dimension, wherein its fascination lies not in the heights of Nobunaga's triumph, but in the depths of failure experienced by the man who lost – Takeda Katsuyori. Nagashino becomes the swan-song of Takeda chivalry, the disaster of a doomed clan that had once been great. Their defeat is so dramatic, so theatrical as to have all the

stuff of grand tragedy about it. It is the ideal myth of the lone samurai warrior, fighting desperately against great odds, transferred from one individual to an entire family.

Son of the Fox-Spirit

Central to the Takeda's tragedy is the pathetic figure of Takeda Katsuyori, Shingen's son and heir. History has not dealt kindly with Katsuyori. He has been represented as headstrong and selfish, an unworthy heir, unwilling to subjugate his own opinions to those wiser counsels provided by the veterans among his father's Twenty-Four Generals. Above all, he is blamed for Nagashino. Kurosawa's film

79

1575
THE BATTLE OF NAGASHINO

Kagemusha, which ends with Nagashino, is particularly dismissive of Katsuyori as it portrays him launching the Takeda cavalry on their last charge. Nagashino is depicted as the Japanese equivalent of the Charge of the Light Brigade, and one is made to ask the simplistic question always posed by any cinemagoer who is both ignorant of Japanese history and bemused by Katsuyori's strange decision. Why did they charge a fence, behind which were thousands of muskets? What, in the case of Nagashino, was 'the reason why?'

To begin to answer this question we must go back many years, to the time in 1544 when Takeda Shingen was expanding his territories from Kai into Shinano province. In 1544 Shingen defeated in battle a local *daimyo* called Suwa Yorishige, and then forced Yorishige to commit suicide following the subsequent humiliating peace conference. Yorishige had a fourteen-year-old daughter of great beauty, whose mother was Shingen's younger sister. She witnessed the defeat of her family and the judicial murder of her father at the hands of the Takeda, and then had to suffer a personal anguish when Shingen became infatuated with her, and took her, his niece, to be one of his wives.

It is not surprising that tongues began to wag. Shingen was so struck with the girl that it was supposed that she was an incarnation of the white fox-spirit of the Suwa Shrine, and had bewitched him in order to gain revenge. Foxes have an important role in Japanese mythology. They can have magical powers, and can readily assume the form of any person or object, often to make mischief with humans. A fox assuming the form of a beautiful woman and making a man fall in love with her is a popular theme in Japanese literature. This 'fox lady' gave birth to Katsuyori in 1546, and died when her son was nine, so that when the destruction of the house came about through Katsuyori, wise old heads nodded and remembered the unhappy circumstances of his birth, and the rumours about his magical mother.

As Shingen had doted on his mother, so he made Katsuyori his favourite son, to the extent of bestowing on him the character 'Yori' in his name, which was common in the Suwa family, rather than 'Nobu', which

he bore himself (as Harunobu) and which his other sons also used. This always set him aside as rather special, and he became heir on the death in 1567 of his elder brother, Yoshinobu, who had been wounded at Kawanakajima. Katsuyori was a capable leader of samurai. He fought well at Kawanakajima, and played a valuable part in the Battle of Mikata-ga-Hara.

Katsuyori's troubles started with the death of his father in 1573. It had been Shingen's recommendation, and earnest wish, that his death be kept secret for three years. In fact the clan managed only two years of deception while Katsuyori and his uncle, Nobukado, kept up a series of campaigns of which Shingen would no doubt have approved. On one occasion, in pursuance of a forward policy against the Tokugawa, and perhaps in a conscious attempt to imitate, or even surpass his late father, Katsuyori raided Ieyasu's province of Totomi along pretty much the same route that Shingen had taken to Mikata-ga-Hara. But this time no army marched out obligingly to meet him, so instead of assaulting the well-defended Hamamatsu, he turned to the north and managed to take the strong castle of Takatenjin, thirty miles further up river, which was a considerable gain for the Takeda and added greatly to Katsuyori's self-confidence.

The border was quiet until 1575, when two things happened. First, Shingen's death was made public with a splendid funeral in April. Second within a few months of Katsuyori's official succession Ieyasu challenged him by making the sensitive appointment of Okudaira Sadamasa (1555–1615) as keeper of Nagashino Castle.

To deal with the person first: the Okudaira were a Mikawa family, and were originally retainers of the Tokugawa, but had been forced to join Shingen. The Takeda can never have been very sure of their loyalty, because Sadamasa's wife and younger brother were kept as permanent hostages, and when Sadamasa rejoined Ieyasu in 1573 by marching his men out of a Takeda castle, Katsuyori had them both crucified. The place in question, Nagashino, was a frontier castle which, together with a number of other fortresses, such as Takatenjin, guarded the entrance into Mikawa and Totomi from the Takeda mountains, much as the similar chain of forts had played their part prior to the Battle of Okehazama. To place a vital fortress under the command of a deadly enemy who was perceived as a traitor was the perfect bait, but would Takeda Katsuyori swallow it?

The Siege of Nagashino

Accounts of the preliminaries to the Battle of Nagashino often portray Katsuyori's advance against the castle as being in itself foolhardy, so that the defeat at the subsequent battle becomes an inevitable consequence of a ridiculous act in the first place. In fact his advance into Totomi was fully in accord with his previously stated objectives, and was nothing out of the ordinary. There is also one extra factor which must be considered. Nagashino was not initially the objective of the fateful advance. What Katsuyori was actually planning was a march on Okazaki, the capital of Mikawa.

The background to this is as follows. There was within the Tokugawa administration in Okazaki a very senior official known as Oga Yashiro. He handled most of the financial affairs of the provinces and was so highly regarded that it was said that the sun

could not rise without Oga Yashiro first giving it permission. In 1575, corrupted perhaps by his position, he turned traitor against the Tokugawa, and offered to open the gates of Okazaki to an advance by the Takeda army. Okazaki Castle was at that time commanded by Ieyasu's son, Nobuyasu, while Ieyasu himself remained at Hamamatsu, and to lose Okazaki, and perhaps all Mikawa too, would lead to the speedy collapse of the Tokugawa. So Takeda Katsuyori set out on his conquest of the Tokugawa along the Iida valley for Okazaki, but while he was on his way the plot was discovered. Oga Yashiro was captured, and sentenced to the slow death of the bamboo saw, whereby the felon was buried up to his neck in the ground with his head protruding through a wooden board. Beside the board was a bamboo saw, which passers-by were invited to take to his neck. He died after seven days. By this time Takeda Katsuyori was well on his way to Okazaki, and had reached the frontier fort of Nagashino, held by the despised Okudaira Sadamasa with only 500 men. Suddenly he heard that his grand scheme had collapsed. Did Katsuyori think he

1575
THE BATTLE OF NAGASHINO

Left: The site of Nagashino Castle. Nagashino was Nobunaga's greatest victory, but was preceded by a long and bitter siege of Nagashino Castle. The castle has never been rebuilt, and its ruins stand on a commanding position overlooking the Toyokawa.

1575
THE BATTLE OF NAGASHINO

Right: Nagashino. This aerial photograph, kindly supplied by Mr Kazukata Ogino, of the Local Government Office of Horai-cho, which includes Nagashino, shows the position of Nagashino Castle where the two rivers meet.

would lose face by retiring? Was the subsequent siege of Nagashino almost a consolation prize, or was it no more than the ideal opportunity to deal with a hated enemy when he had ready for battle and high on adrenalin a 15,000-man samurai army? Whatever Katsuyori's immediate motive Nagashino soon became his Verdun, a fortress of which the capture would be as much symbolic as it was strategic. The siege having begun, Takeda Katsuyori was unwilling to allow it to finish without the castle's capitulation. Do we detect from this a certain lack of confidence, compared with how his father had behaved before Hamamatsu in 1572, when he retired to fight better another day? Nagashino had changed hands before, but that fact gives

little indication of how desperately it could be defended, and attacked, when the motivation was there.

Nagashino was a naturally strong place, as illustrated in the photographs on pages 45 and 47. It was built on a rocky promontory where the Onogawa and the Takigawa join to become the Toyokawa, forming a letter 'Y', the stem of which is pointing almost due south. The author has closely examined the site which, being in a country district, is little changed from 1575. The rivers are almost 100 yards wide, with high rocky banks. Nowadays the banks are covered with trees, as shown by the view on page 45 which is taken from the modern road bridge across the Toyokawa, but in 1575 all the trees on the attackers' side

would have been cut down to allow a good field of view. The only open ground is to the north, which the defenders strengthened with the usual ditches and palisades. It is also surrounded to the south and east (across the river) by mountains, which give a good vantage-point on the castle. An attacking commander could therefore control his troops very accurately when carrying out an assault. Katsuyori, however, sited his main *honjin*, his headquarters post, to the flatter land north of the castle, where communications with Kai would be easier.

The attacks on Nagashino began on 16 June 1575. Following a few assaults to test the defenders' mettle the Takeda attempted to dig mines under the northern defences.

In this context the term 'mines' almost certainly means tunnels to allow troops entry, rather than saps for explosive devices, though the latter are not beyond the bounds of possibility. It is unlikely that much stone was used in the fort's construction, so there would have been little to bring crashing down from a European-style mining operation. The Takeda did have the finest miners in Japan, as their territory contained several gold-mines, so it is not surprising to hear of such techniques being used. The defenders, however, succeeded in countermining them.

From the opposite banks of the rivers waterborne attacks from rafts were mounted. Such operations are always hazardous and the defenders had little difficulty in overturning them. A general assault was then made by the Takeda army, but once again the place held out. At this point Takeda Katsuyori decided on a long siege. Outside the defenders' palisades the attackers erected a further palisade of their own to bottle them up. Thick ropes were stretched across the rivers to block the other possible exit routes, and the Takeda army sat down to starve out the stubborn Okudaira Sadamasa.

Torii Suneemon

Every battle in samurai history remembers at least one figure for a particular act of heroism. At Nagashino it was Torii Suneemon, who escaped from the beleaguered castle and took a message to Ieyasu.

Both Nobunaga and Ieyasu were already aware of the castle's plight. They knew that the defenders had only enough food for about four or five days. Some of Nobunaga's senior officers had advised against sending a relieving force, and the issue was only settled by what looks suspiciously like self-interest. If troops were not sent from Nobunaga to help a Tokugawa captain, Ieyasu might ally himself with the Takeda, they reasoned. So the alliance held. Nobunaga had left Gifu on the 13th, and arrived at Okazaki the following day. Ieyasu had moved to Okazaki, it being nearer the scene of the action than Hamamatsu.

As their conference proceeded over the next couple of days their minds were concentrated by the arrival of Torii Suneemon.

1575
THE BATTLE OF NAGASHINO

1575
THE BATTLE OF
NAGASHINO

Right: Torii Suneemon. Torii Suneemon was a samurai of the Nagashino Castle guard. He volunteered to take a message to Nobunaga, and swam along the river through the nets the Takeda had stretched across it. He was eventually captured and crucified, but not until after the warning had got through to Nobunaga, which resulted in the Battle of Nagashino. This modern painting of him is in the Nagashino Castle Preservation Hall.

A Mikawa retainer, he had volunteered to slip out of the castle through the Takeda lines and deliver the urgent message that immediate relief was needed. He swam down the river on the night of 22 June, cutting the hawsers with his sharp dagger, and on the following morning made a signal to the garrison to indicate that he was on his way to Okazaki. Some sources say he lit a bonfire on Mount Gambo, others that he let off a signal rocket. His message was that they had plenty of ammunition, that morale was high, but that they could only hold out for another two or three days. Nobunaga was most impressed, and promised to start the following day.

Torii returned to Mount Gambo and lit three fires as a signal, but this time the Takeda were ready for him. They had repaired the hawsers and tied bells to them, and spread soft sand along the riverbank to betray any tell-tale footprints. Torii Suneemon was apprehended and brought before Katsuyori who offered him a deal. If he would tell the garrison that no help was forthcoming and they might as well surrender, his life would be spared and he would be taken into the service of the Takeda. Suneemon let Katsuyori think he was in agreement, but Katsuyori took no chances, and made him report the false message from the Takeda-occupied bank.

Some sources say he was already bound to a cross, to be crucified if he failed to behave as the Takeda desired, others that he stood on the bank. But instead of urging surrender he shouted, 'Hold fast. Help will soon be at hand!' and was immediately put to death.

Torii's sacrifice impressed friend and enemy alike. One retainer of the Takeda was so impressed that he and Torii became 'blood-brothers' while he was still on the cross, and had a banner painted of him which he used henceforth in battle. All we know of this admirer was that his name was Saiheiji. There is a copy of the banner in Nagashino Castle Museum. The site of Torii's crucifixion is marked today by a monument. It is directly across the river from the castle site, well within shouting distance, but the effect is spoiled by the thick forest on the bank.

Shitarabara

Torii Suneemon's defiant goods news to the defenders of the castle was also valuable intelligence to Takeda Katsuyori, who now knew for certain that a relieving force was on its way, and that it was likely to be a formidable one. The estimates were that the Takeda force of 15,000 would be opposed by an allied Oda/Tokugawa army of 38,000. Katsuyori held council with

Left: Baba Nobuharu. Baba Nobuharu had formerly been one of Shingen's Twenty-Four Generals, and was one of many senior Takeda retainers killed at Nagashino. Behind him is Saigusa Moritomo, who also died.

his senior officers and considerable differences of opinion were expressed. Shingen's veterans, such as Baba Nobuharu, Naito Masatoyo, Yamagata Masakage and Oyamada Nobushige, who had belonged to the Twenty-Four Generals, were for making an honourable withdrawal. The younger ones were for fighting, men like Atobe Oi-no-suke, who scorned the advice of their elders and called it a disgrace. The tragedy of the Takeda was that Katsuyori listened to this advice.

Soon even the old generals had to accept that Katsuyori was determined to meet Nobunaga in battle. Baba Nobuharu, levelheaded as ever, suggested that if there was going to be a fight it should be conducted from within Nagashino Castle and a determined effort to take the fortress should be made before the allied army arrived. There was a garrison of five hundred, he reasoned, and even if an assault were met by a hail of arrows and bullets it should be possible to overwhelm them, even at considerable loss, by sheer weight of numbers. But that too smacked of cowardice to the young bucks. The Takeda would meet them in a pitched battle the following morning. The old generals had followed Shingen loyally, and had transferred that tremendous loyalty to his son. Their duty now meant that they must die with him. Four of

the old Twenty-Four, Baba Nobuharu, Naito Masatoyo, Yamagata Masakage and Tsuchiya Masatsugu exchanged a symbolic farewell cup of water.

The eve of the battle was not a peaceful one for the Takeda camp. Before dawn the Takeda experienced a little more of the considerable expertise the Mikawa forces seem to have enjoyed in night attacks, when Sakai Tadatsugu, one of the heroes of the retreat at Mikata-ga Hara, led 3,000 men in a raid on the Takeda camp, similar to the one they had carried out at Saigadake. This attack was very successful indeed, because they managed to kill the sector commander, Takeda Nobuzane, who was Katsuyori's uncle, and one of two surviving younger brothers of Shingen present at Nagashino. This was a grave loss to the Takeda, and a foretaste of what was to come.

On the morning of 29 June 1575, Takeda Katsuyori led a charge of the Takeda samurai against Nobunaga's field fortifications on Shitarabara, and the rest, as they say, is history. The Takeda horsemen were shot down by 3,000 arquebuses, and finished off by the Oda samurai. The film *Kagemusha*, which for most people is all they know of Nagashino, shows dramatically the effect of the tactics employed by Nobunaga on this occasion; how he

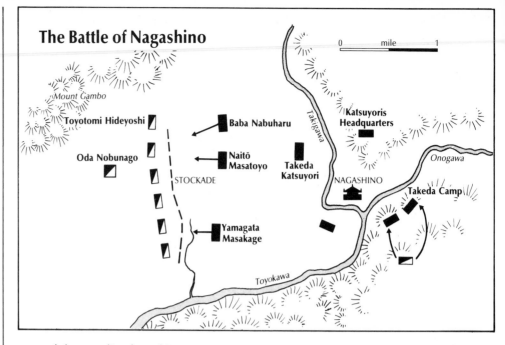

The Battle of Nagashino

Mount Gambo

Toyotomi Hideyoshi

Oda Nobunago

STOCKADE

Baba Nabuharu

Naitō Masatoyo

Takeda Katsuyori

Yamagata Masakage

Katsuyoris Headquarters

Takigawa

Onogawa

NAGASHINO

Takeda Camp

Toyokawa

0   mile   1

erected fences, lined up his 3,000 arquebusiers, and fired volleys that brought
down the Takeda cavalry in scores. That is
the popular view of Nagashino, but let us
examine the situation at Shitarabara more
closely.

Shitarabara, the plain where the Takeda
charged the Oda army, is not the flat, open
grassland shown in *Kagemusha*. It is hilly,
and crossed by streams, and extends to the
foothills of Mount Gambo. The palisade
Nobunaga erected was about a mile from
Nagashino Castle. As to the question of
Takeda Katsuyori as a leader of a 'Charge of
the Light Brigade' – it must be emphasized
that the Takeda charge was not a reaction to
the fence and the gunners. The fence and
the gunners were Oda Nobunaga's innova-
tive response to the likelihood of a Takeda
charge, which he and Tokugawa Ieyasu
knew could be utterly devastating. It had
worked at Ueda-hara in 1548 against the
Murakami, and it had worked against their
own troops at Mikata-ga-Hara only three
years previously. These mounted samurai,
the decisive arm of the Takeda army, who
attacked 'Swift as the wind, as fierce as fire
and as silent as a forest' according to the
great clan banner, had been outwitted by
Uesugi Kenshin only by very clever manoeuvring at the Fourth Battle of Kawanakajima. Nobunaga had no night-time manoeuvring to rely upon. The Takeda had

decided to fight him in the open where
their traditional techniques might be used
to their best effect.

Oda Nobunaga's great achievement at
Nagashino was to out-think Katsuyori in his
preparations. To reach his lines the Takeda
would have to cross two streams which
flowed into the Toyokawa (see map on page
86). This would slow them down anyway, so
behind the second of these he erected his
loose palisade. It was certainly not a con-
tinuous fence, and probably not in one
straight line, because he had to provide the
means whereby his samurai could deliver a
counter-attack once the streams, the palisades and the arquebusiers had slowed
down the charge sufficiently to allow the
Oda and Tokugawa samurai to meet the
Takeda on equal terms. That was as much as
Nobunaga could reasonably hope from his
arrangement. Anything more would be a
bonus, but merely to break the rhythm of
the charge would probably be sufficient.
Somehow the dreadful impact of those
mighty horsemen had to be reduced to a
minimum, and Nobunaga's great innova-
tion at Nagashino was that he trusted his
lowly *ashigaru* to bring it about. The sharp
blades of the samurai would settle the
victory, but the despised *ashigaru* were to
put it into their hands.

In fact it is evident that much more was
achieved by the arquebus fire than merely

1575
THE BATTLE OF NAGASHINO

Left: The arquebuses bring down the Takeda cavalry. In this scene from the copy of the Nagashino screen the arquebuses of Oda Nobunaga's army bring down the vanguard of the Takeda. The white mon on black identify the fallen as men of Yamagata.

七

1575
THE BATTLE OF NAGASHINO

Right: Arquebuses at the Nagashino Festival. Every year the Battle of Nagashino is commemorated by the Nagashino Banner Festival, which features the firing of arquebuses. The photograph is of the 1986 festival, which was marred by heavy rain. Nevertheless most of the firearms worked, with deafening results. The gunners are in the costume of the Edo Period.

Right: The fence at Shitarabara. A small section of the palisade at Nagashino has been reproduced at the site of the Takeda charge, a place called Shitarabara.

breaking the charge. Most accounts of Nagashino credit Nobunaga's *ashigaru* with rotational volley firing in three ranks, and this is not beyond the bounds of possibility. Nobunaga's disciplining of his *ashigaru* was one of his best achievements, and placed him ahead of nearly all his contemporaries. One might argue that he

would have had to have volley firing in order to keep up the rate of firing which the chronicles report. But how effective was it? We know that 10,000 casualties were sustained on the Takeda side, including a number of the Takedas' ablest generals who died during the battle, but it is open to conjecture as to how many actually died from the fire at the palisade, and how many fell victim to the swords and spears of the samurai.

It is also interesting to note that a chronicle called the *Nagashino Jisenki* ('true account of the Battle of Nagashino'), records that Takeda Katsuyori was fully aware before the battle began that Nobunaga had many arquebuses, and was relying on the heavy rain which the area had been experiencing to render them useless. A weapon that works by means of a smouldering match falling on to an open pan must be very vulnerable to bad weather, as was demonstrated to the author during the *Nagashino kassen nobori matsuri*, the annual festival held at Nagashino each May. The weather in 1986 was dreadful, and during the half-hour demonstration of arquebus fire approximately 40 per cent of shots did not fire.

The morning of the battle, however, dawned bright and clear, and the matches were dry when the charge began at 5 a.m. Not everyone in Nobunaga's army was behind the famous palisade when the fighting started. Nobunaga had placed a detachment of men under Okubo Tadayo outside the stockade as 'bait', and these drew an attack from about 2,000 Takeda samurai under Yamagata Masakage and other leaders. This was on the Takeda left. On the right Baba Nobuharu attacked Sakuma Morimasa, who drew Baba on with a feigned retreat. This was successful, and Baba's men triumphantly occupied a small hillock, from which they launched an attack on the stockade. Here the arquebus volleys drove them back, and samurai under the command of Toyotomi Hideyoshi and Shibata Katsuie attacked them in flank and rear.

Katsuyori then ordered a full-scale attack along the line, committing all his reserves in one desperate effort. Once again the attack was slowed to nothing, and Oda Nobunaga advanced his men through the

1575
THE BATTLE OF NAGASHINO

Left: Ramming an arquebus. One of the participants in the 1986 Nagashino Banner Festival rams the powder and wad down the barrel of his arquebus.

七

1575
THE BATTLE OF NAGASHINO

Right: The defenders sally out of Nagashino Castle. Once the Takeda samurai were seen to be broken the defenders of Nagashino Castle attacked them in the rear.

palisade to attack the swordsmen on their own terms. By midday it was clear that the battle was lost, and Baba Nobuharu, who had somehow survived the charge, forced Katsuyori to retreat from the field. Baba Nobuharu covered his retreat as he headed north for about three miles, and held off the enemy until Katsuyori was able to cross the Kansagawa. Baba Nobuharu was then overwhelmed and killed.

The Takeda lost 10,000 men (65 per cent) in the battle, while the allied army lost 6,000 (15 per cent). Quite a great difference in number, and a great difference also in the quality of the troops. Seven of the remaining Takeda Twenty-Four Generals were killed. They were Baba Nobuharu, who was killed covering Katsuyori's retreat; Hara Masatane, an expert at strategy; Sanada Nobutsuna, who cut deeply into the Oda ranks before being overwhelmed along with his younger brother, Masateru; Yamagata Masakage, one of Shingen's most trusted generals; Saigusa Moritomo, Masakage's nephew, who had done well at Mikata-ga-Hara; Tsuchiya Masatsugu, who had also fought at Mikata-ga-Hara and whose family were destined to be Katsuyori's last supporters; and Naito Masatoyo, whose charge at Mikata-ga-Hara is illustrated on page 72. Obata Masamori later died from a wound received during the Nagashino campaign. There were numerous other high-ranking casualties.

Temmoku-zan

It would be wrong to leave the discussion of Nagashino without giving a brief account of the following seven years, which ended with Katsuyori's death. After such a defeat it is surprising to note that the Takeda clan limped on for so long, but Kai and Shinano were easier to defend than the coastal provinces of Mikawa and Totomi. In 1578 their great rival, Uesugi Kenshin, died, and a succession dispute within the family took a lot of pressure off the Takeda from this direction. Between 1575 and 1581 Tokugawa Ieyasu conducted a series of operations against Katsuyori, which resulted in the regaining of Takatenjin Castle early in 1581. By this time even Katsuyori's own subjects were beginning to lose confidence in him, and in 1581 he alienated many by building a new castle, Shimpu-jo, near Nirasaki, and

1575
THE BATTLE OF NAGASHINO

七

1575
THE BATTLE OF NAGASHINO

Right: The last stand of the Tsuchiya brothers. The Tsuchiya clan, one of whose members had been one of Takeda Shingen's Twenty-Four Generals, stood by Katsuyori to the end. In this scene from the *Ehon Taiko-ki* they defend Katsuyori from attack, allowing him time to commit suicide on Temmoku-zan.

proclaiming it as his new capital. Shingen had never relied on a fortified place as his capital. Tsutsuji-ga-saki, his headquarters in Kofu, had been a simple *hirajiro* with one moat. Now his heir was seeking refuge behind stone walls!

The following year one of the major Takeda vassals revolted. This was Kiso Yoshimasa, who was apparently descended from Kiso Yoshinaka, the victor of Kurikara, and held the castle of Kiso-Fukushima on the Nakasendo, almost at the limit of Takeda territory. In 1582 the combined forces of Oda and Tokugawa turned against the Takeda. (To follow the campaign see the map on page 42, which shows the Takeda territories.) Nobunaga's son, Oda Nobutada, invaded Shinano, and one by one the Takeda allies collapsed before them. Even Anayama Baisetsu, who had

been one of Shingen's Twenty-Four Generals, left Katsuyori for the obviously winning side.

Only his closest relatives stood by him. A younger brother, Morinobu, who had been adopted into the Nishina family, held out valiantly at Takato Castle, along the route which his father had taken to Mikata-ga-Hara. Then Ieyasu struck northwards into Kai. Katsuyori burned his new castle of Shimpu-jo and fled to the most distant mountains of his territory. Oyamada Nobushige, one of the old Twenty-Four who had survived Nagashino, had offered him refuge in his castle of Iwadono, but when Katsuyori arrived he found the gates shut against him. By now his army had shrunk to 300 men. The only famous name from the Twenty-Four who remained with him to the last was the family of Tsuchiya.

Nagashino Today

As the area is rural and unspoiled, Nagashino is one of the most rewarding battlefields to visit. Take the Japan National Railways Tokaido line to Toyohashi (a journey which can be made by the *Shinkansen* 'bullet train'), and then change to the J.N.R. Iida line for Toyokawa. Most trains terminate at Toyokawa, so you will have to change for Nagashino. If you have time it is worth making a detour to see the magnificent Toyokawa Inari Shrine, before leaving for Nagashino. The train goes across the battlefield, and through the castle ruins! The next station is Nagashino-jo (Nagashino Castle) and gives you a walk of about half a mile back to the site. There is a splendid museum, the 'Nagashino Castle Preservation Hall', which contains models, armour and documents relating to the battle, including photographs of the Nagashino screen. After exploring the castle site, walk across the bridge and pay your respects at the site of Torii Suneemon's crucifixion, then double back slightly to appreciate the steep cliffs of the rivers' confluence from the road bridge. From here you can walk the mile to Shitarabara, where the local council has erected a reproduction of a section of the palisade. Rejoin the Toyokawa train at Mikawatogo.

The best time to visit Nagashino is in May: the first and second Sundays are the usual dates for the Nagashino Festival. It is an unforgettable experience to stand in the old courtyard of the castle and hear arquebus fire echoing from the surrounding hills.

A visit to Temmoku-zan, site of Katsuyori's last stand, is straightforward, if a little remote, and is best combined with a visit to the Takeda 'sites' of Kofu. Take the local train out of Kofu heading east. Enzan is the stop if you wish to visit Shingen's temple of repose, the Erin-ji, where there is a new museum in which, among other fascinating memorabilia, are kept the old Takeda flags (the guidebooks still say they are in the Unpo-ji). A few stations further on is Hajikano. From Hajikano station it is a walk of about a mile to Torii-bata and the Keitoku-In, where you may see Katsuyori's grave. If you are lucky with the weather your trip will be rewarded by the 'connoisseur's view' of Mount Fuji from the north, visible for much of the train journey.

田野の天目山々はないく武田主従末期の合戦

The three sons of Tsuchiya Masatsugu, who had been killed at Nagashino, fought with Katsuyori and his son Nobukatsu at their last battle at Torii-bata, a pass overlooked by a mountain called Temmoku-zan, by which name the battle is usually known. There were thirty survivors. While the Tsuchiya brothers held the enemy back, Katsuyori's young wife, aged nineteen, committed suicide by stabbing herself. Katsuyori, acting as her second, cut off her head, then with his son committed *hara-kiri*.

So died the unfortunate Takeda Katsuyori, the man who had supposedly been born as an act of revenge by a fox disguised as a beautiful woman. He is buried within walking distance of the place where he died, a tragic figure in Japanese history, the heir who inherited, but did not succeed.

1575
THE BATTLE OF NAGASHINO

Right: Temmoku-zan. The mountain of Temmoku, seen from the pass of Torii-bata deep in the hills of Kai, marks the end of the Takeda. At Torii-bata, Katsuyori fought his last battle. He is buried nearby at the Keitoku-In.

1583

The Battle of Shizugatake

With the Battle of Shizugatake we have moved almost into another world. Shingen is dead, his son Katsuyori is dead and, most importantly – because it was the ultimate reason why the battle was fought – Oda Nobunaga is dead.

The Honno-ji Incident

Oda Nobunaga may have been invincible in battle, but he was not immune against the treacherous attack or the silent assassin. He was customarily surrounded by a very large bodyguard, a sensible precaution at any time in Japanese history, but when his end came it was brought about from within the ranks of his own army.

Nobunaga's army was the classic model of the retainer band, based on the pattern he had inherited from his father, whereby his vassals were organized according to the closeness of their family ties and the loyalty they gave to the family. Apart from the *ichizoku-shu*, the family members, who consisted of his three sons, Nobutada, Nobuo and Nobukata, and six brothers, his retainers were either *fudai*, 'inner' or *tozama*, 'outer' vassals. His chief retainer overall, his *shukuro*, was Shibata Katsuie, of whom we shall hear much in this chapter. He had command of the other *fudai*, the *go-umawari-shu* (the bodyguard) and all the *tozama* vassals, some of whom had been conquered by Nobunaga and submitted, and others whose loyalty was possibly open to question. Among them was a man called Akechi Mitsuhide.

Akechi Mitsuhide (1526–82) had begun his military service with the Saito of Mino province, and then joined Nobunaga. He proved to be an excellent leader, and was rewarded in 1571 with the castle of Sakamoto and a revenue of 100,000 *koku*. During the late 1570s he was one of the retainers entrusted with the unglamorous job of pacifying the western end of Honshu. Mitsuhide concentrated on the northern provinces of the area, Toyotomi Hideyoshi on the southern. In 1582 Hide-yoshi was engaged in the long and complicated siege of Takamatsu Castle, which was eventually only reduced by flooding, when the news came to him that Akechi Mitsuhide had set off with a large army from Kyoto to bring him reinforcements, then had turned round on the outskirts of the capital, and with the order 'The enemy is in the Honno-ji', had descended suddenly upon Nobunaga and his bodyguard in the Honno-ji temple where they were staying. There had been a violent skirmish, and as the temple blazed around him the mortally wounded Nobunaga had committed *hara-kiri*. Mitsuhide's men had then stormed the Nijo Palace and killed Nobunaga's eldest son, Nobutada.

Mitsuhide's motives for turning against his master, Oda Nobunaga, and having him murdered, have been much discussed. It has been suggested that Nobunaga was jealous of Mitsuhide's skills as a poet, and spared no excuse to humiliate him, and that Nobunaga had tried to have Mitsuhide murdered. The author inclines more towards the circumstantial evidence supplied by an incident in 1577. At this time Akechi Mitsuhide was conducting a campaign in Tamba province to the north-west of Kyoto, and laid siege to Yagami Castle, which was owned by Hatano Hideharu. It was a long siege, so to persuade Hatano to surrender, Mitsuhide somehow managed to obtain his mother as hostage, whereupon Hatano submitted. The taking of hostages was a common enough practice, and must be regarded in this case as a sensible move on Mitsuhide's part. Unfortunately, when Hatano was taken before Nobunaga he ordered him to be crucified, even though both he and Mitsuhide had kept their bargain. Mitsuhide was furious, and more so when the surviving retainers of Hatano blamed Mitsuhide for their lord's death, and seized his mother as hostage. (One is forced to conclude that samurai warlords were rather careless over the accommodation they provided for aged

八

1583
THE BATTLE OF SHIZUGATAKE

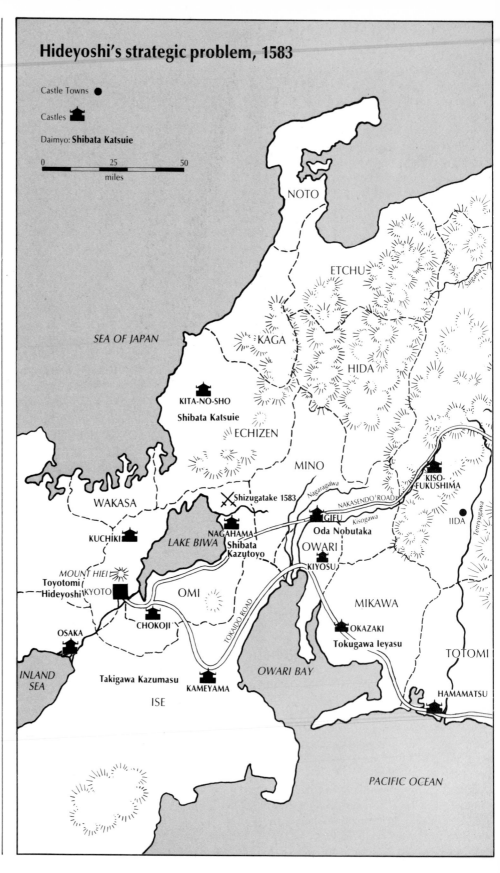

Hideyoshi's strategic problem, 1583

Castle Towns ●

Castles ♟

Daimyo: **Shibata Katsuie**

0   25   50
miles

NOTO

ETCHU

SEA OF JAPAN

KAGA

HIDA

KITA-NO-SHO

Shibata Katsuie

ECHIZEN

MINO

KISO-
FUKUSHIMA

✗ Shizugatake 1583

Nagaragawa

NAKASENDO ROAD

IIDA

WAKASA

Tennugawa

KUCHIKI

LAKE BIWA

NAGAHAMA
**Shibata
Kazutoyo**

GIFU
Oda Nobutaka

Kisogawa

OWARI

MOUNT HIEI
**Toyotomi
Hideyoshi** KYOTO

KIYOSU

OMI

MIKAWA

CHOKOJI

TOKAIDO ROAD

OKAZAKI
Tokugawa Ieyasu

OSAKA

*INLAND
SEA*

TOTOMI

Takigawa Kazumasu

KAMEYAMA

OWARI BAY

HAMAMATSU

ISE

PACIFIC OCEAN

parents). The unfortunate lady was hung by her ankles from a tree and murdered, an incident which is supposed to have fired in Mitsuhide the resentment against Nobunaga that smouldered for five years until the absence from Kyoto of most of Nobunaga's army gave him the opportunity to strike.

Yamazaki

There were few greater honours to be won in Medieval Japan than to become the avenger of one's dead master. The classic story of the Forty-Seven Ronin is the best-

known example, and once Nobunaga was dead his retainers practically fell over themselves for the honour of taking Mitsuhide's head, and reaping the rewards that would surely follow. Toyotomi Hideyoshi was the first to be informed. He kept the news secret, and rapidly drew up generous terms with the Mori clan, whose castle he was besieging. He then marched his army back to Kyoto as quickly as possible and fought Akechi Mitsuhide at the Battle of Yamazaki, midway between Kyoto and Osaka. Mitsuhide was soundly defeated, and murdered by a group of peasants as he fled

1583
THE BATTLE OF SHIZUGATAKE

Left: Toyotomi Hideyoshi. This scene from the *Ehon Taiko-ki* depicts the hero of that work, Toyotomi Hideyoshi, in field camp. His paulownia *mon* appears on the *maku* which surround his camp, and he is flying his 'golden gourd' standard.

1583
THE BATTLE OF
SHIZUGATAKE

Right: Shibata Katsuie smashes the water-jars. Shibata Katsuie is today chiefly remembered for being the loser at the Battle of Shizugatake, but he was in fact a very able general, and Oda Nobunga's most senior retainer. He gained great glory at the siege of Chokoji in 1570. Once the aqueduct to Chokoji had been cut, Shibata's men faced a slow death from thirst. In front of his entire garrison Shibata took his spear and smashed the jars containing their last remaining water, shouting 'Sooner a quick death in battle than a slow death from thirst.' He then led his men in a desperate charge, which carried the day and saved the castle.

wounded from the field. This gave Hideyoshi a tremendous advantage in any future negotiations over Nobunaga's succession.

Others were not so decisive, and the case of Tsutsui Junkei (1549–84) is positively comic. He was related to Akechi Mitsuhide, and brought his troops to assist him at Yamazaki, but noting the great strength of Hideyoshi's army he kept his own army waiting beside the pass of Hora-ga-toge to see how the fight would go. Once Hideyoshi was seen to be victorious he joined in on the winning side. His action is remembered today in the Japanese expression 'to wait on Hora-ga-toge', the Japanese equivalent of 'sitting on the fence'!

The essence of Mitsuhide's plot against Nobunaga had been that it should be carried out when all, or at least the majority, of Nobunaga's senior retainers and allies were otherwise engaged. Nobunaga's most senior retainer, his *shukuro*, Shibata Katsuie, was heavily committed far to the north of Kyoto, and was not able to reach the capital until Yamazaki had been fought, and monkey-faced little Hideyoshi, whom Nobunaga had originally recruited as an *ashigaru*, was proclaiming his *fait accompli*. It was quite intolerable.

Shibata Katsuie

Shibata Katsuie is one of the great losers of Medieval Japan. In common with Imagawa Yoshimoto and Takeda Katsuyori he is best-known for losing his last battle, rather than for the series of victories that preceded it. Let us begin by putting the record straight.

His family were hereditary vassals of the Oda, and Katsuie fought for Oda Nobuhide and later for his son Nobunaga. His greatest achievement came in 1570, in a little-known incident which deserves retelling. Shibata Katsuie was entrusted with the defence of Chokoji Castle in Omi province, a *yamashiro* built on a hill just to the south of Lake Biwa. This strategic position, which overlooked the section of the Tokaido where it is the same road as the Nakasendo, was besieged by the father and son team of Rokkaku Yoshikata and Rokkaku Yoshisuke, with 4,000 men. All castles are dependent on a good water supply, and Chokoji was fed by a wooden aqueduct that was kept closely guarded. The Rokkaku troops succeeded in smashing the aqueduct, and waited for Shibata's garrison of 400 to succumb to thirst and surrender. To keep up morale among his troops, and to mislead the enemy into thinking they were prospering, Shibata Katsuie kept sending samurai out to the Rokkaku lines to make wild attacks and then withdraw, but one was captured, and, exhausted, cried out for water. The enemy then knew that the garrison had very little water left, and prepared for a sudden assault when they were weakened. That night Shibata Katsuie gathered all his men into the inner courtyard of the castle, and showed them the three remaining water jars which held enough to last them one more day. Then, in full view of his army, Katsuie astounded them by taking his spear and smashing its blade into the jars, so that all the precious water ran out. 'Sooner a quick death in battle than a slow death from thirst!' he shouted, and led his army out of the gates in a last desperate charge against the Rokkaku. So vigorously did they fight that they carried all before them and gained a totally unexpected victory.

Following the victory of the Anegawa, Shibata was granted the Asakura territories of Echizen and Kaga provinces, and made his capital at a castle called Kita-no-sho, which is now the city of Fukui. He also gained one further reward: the wife of Asai Nagamasa, Nobunaga's sister. Strange to relate she had previously been married to Shibata Katsuie, but had then been married to Asai Nagamasa, by whom she had the three daughters previously referred to.

From Echizen and Kaga, Katsuie began to expand northwards to the Noto peninsula, and the local *daimyo* appealed for help to Uesugi Kagekatsu, who had inherited the domains of his adoptive father, Uesugi Kenshin. Katsuie was preparing to fight the mighty Uesugi when news came of Nobunaga's death. He hurried back, to find Nobunaga avenged and the appointment of a successor being fiercely disputed.

The Rivals
At the time of his death Nobunaga had five sons. The youngest, Katsunaga, was killed with him at the Honno-ji, and the eldest, Nobutada, was killed shortly afterwards at the Nijo Palace. The fourth, Hidekatsu, was fifteen years old and was adopted by Toyotomi Hideyoshi. That left two men in their twenties, Nobuo and Nobutaka, and a one-year-old grandson, the son of Nobutaka, called Samboshi. At the con-

ference called to decide the succession, the baby Samboshi was finally declared as Nobunaga's heir, with his uncle and his father as his guardians. Disputes soon arose between the guardians, and Toyotomi Hideyoshi cleverly manipulated them and those of his comrades who declared an interest one way or another.

Each brother was in one of Nobunaga's old castles: Nobuo in Kiyosu, and Nobutaka in Gifu. Hideyoshi favoured Nobuo's cause, while his strongest rivals, Takigawa and Shibata Katsuie, favoured Nobutaka. It was soon very obvious to all concerned that Toyotomi Hideyoshi, avenger of Nobunaga, intended to rule through this infant, and inherit by default. If the rest of Nobunaga's former comrades had been able to unite successfully against him they would have been able easily to defeat him. But co-operation was not their strong point, and Hideyoshi was counting on their failure to act together, and his ability to play one off against another.

Hideyoshi's strategic position was very weak. He was entirely surrounded by three hostile forces: Nobutaka in Gifu, which effectively controlled his movements along the Tokaido; Takigawa Kazumasu in Kameyama in Ise province, very inconveniently situated on the Tokaido; and Shibata to the north. All Hideyoshi's routes from the capital other than to the west were controlled by these three enemy armies.

The Shizugatake Campaign
It was to Hideyoshi's advantage that he did not have to fight three armies at once, because the foolish Oda Nobutaka very cleverly decided to attack Hideyoshi while Shibata's army was still snowbound in Echizen province and unable to help him. So Hideyoshi first turned his attentions towards Oda Nobutaka in Gifu, and attacked him with the blessing of Oda Nobuo. His reputation for success in siege-work was such that Nobutaka immediately surrendered.

On arriving back in Kyoto, Hideyoshi was informed that Takigawa, in Kameyama, had been forced into action by Nobutaka's precipitate challenge, and was planning a joint assault from two directions, helped by Shibata's son, Kazutoyo, who held Naga-hama Castle in Omi, the fortress Hideyoshi

1583
THE BATTLE OF SHIZUGATAKE

had been given after Anegawa. Being much further south than Kita-no-sho, Nagahama was free of snow. So Hideyoshi headed for Nagahama, and bought its surrender with a handsome bribe. Fearing a thaw, which would bring Shibata's mighty army advancing from Echizen, Hideyoshi set off immediately to Kameyama and laid siege to it. Takigawa surrendered to him when mines began to collapse the walls.

But the greatest threat was to come with the spring of 1583. In the chapter on the Battle of the Anegawa we noted how there were two possible routes an army could take from Echizen province to attack Kyoto. One was west of Lake Biwa, past Mount Hiei, the other was east of the lake, to join the Nakasendo. To guard against Shibata's advance by either route, Hideyoshi constructed a series of forts on the mountain peaks at Lake Biwa's northern tip, where a number of hills divide Lake Biwa from its little sister Lake Yogo. The farthest north of the chain was Iwasaki-yama, in which Hideyoshi installed as keeper Takayama Ukon, and next to it was Oiwa, while a few miles to the south was Tagami, under Hideyoshi's half-brother, Hashiba Hidenaga, overlooking the main road and the site of the present-day town of Kinomoto. Midway between the two lakes, and on one of the highest peaks, sat Nakagawa Kiyohide, in a fortress called Shizugatake.

The Battle of Shizugatake

The frontier forts remained quiet as the snow began to melt, and Hideyoshi's attentions were once again drawn to Gifu. Oda Nobutaka had revolted again, so Hideyoshi began a further siege of this stronghold, from a base at the castle of Ogaki on the Nakasendo. But it was to prove a blessing in disguise, because it took Hideyoshi that much nearer to the frontier with Echizen. He had no sooner begun siege operations when news came that Shibata Katsuie had sent his nephew, Sakuma Morimasa, on into Omi to secure these frontier forts. It had gone well for Sakuma. Iwasakiyama had fallen, and its commander had withdrawn to Tagami. Sakuma had then besieged Shizugatake, which had not fallen, although its commander, Nakagawa Kiyohide, had been killed. The messenger added that the siege was continuing.

The Battle of Shizugatake

The siege was continuing . . . Sakuma Morimasa had not withdrawn to the security of one of the captured forts, but had built loose siege lines round Shizugatake! Did he not know that Hideyoshi's army was only at Ogaki, from which the forts could be reached speedily along some of the best roads in Japan? Hideyoshi acted quickly, and set off from Ogaki with as large a mounted force as he could muster, to gallop the fifty miles to Shizugatake.

Sakuma Morimasa was at the head of 15,000 troops, and ten hours previously had enjoyed a considerable success by capturing the fort on the summit of Oiwayama, and ensuring the death of Hideyoshi's commander, Nakagawa Kiyohide, in the next fort along. His uncle Shibata Katsuie's orders had been quite precise. 'Don't underestimate "Monkey-face". He's a fellow to whom carelessness is unknown. If you succeed in capturing Oiwa withdraw your troops into it.'

Morimasa did in fact know that Hideyoshi had made camp at Ogaki in order to take Gifu, and calculated, not unreasonably, that it would take at least three days to move his 20,000 men to Shizugatake. By this time the confident Sakuma Morimasa would have captured it. As a result he chose to disobey Shibata's orders and concentrated on capturing one further prize.

That night Sakuma Morimasa looked down towards the eastern foot of Shizugatake to see the valley become a sea of fire from thousands of pine torches. Helped,

1583
THE BATTLE OF
SHIZUGATAKE

Left: The Seven Spears Memorial. The memorial of the Battle of Shizugatake takes the form of this attractive statue of a sleeping samurai on the summit of Shizugatake.

八

1583
THE BATTLE OF
SHIZUGATAKE

Right: Sakuma Morimasa captures Oiwa. This vigorous illustration depicts Shibata Katsuie's nephew Sakuma Morimasa capturing Hideyoshi's frontier fortress of Oiwa. He then disobeyed Shibata's orders to remain in Oiwa, and was defeated at the Battle of Shizugatake.

no doubt, by fresh horses procured at Nagahama on the way, Hideyoshi's army had arrived in less than one day. His army linked up with the defenders of Tagami, while Sakuma Morimasa hurriedly changed his plans, and ordered his men to abandon their siege lines and take up a defensive position against Hideyoshi's attack.

Leading Hideyoshi's vanguard was an enthusiastic young warrior (or *wakamusha* to use the splendidly sounding Japanese term) called Kato Kiyomasa, eager to take part in his first major encounter. This flamboyant character, who was to make his mark on samurai history over the next three decades, was a native of Owari province,

and was born in 1562 in Nakamura, the same village that had produced Hideyoshi. He was the son of the village blacksmith, and his mother was somehow related to Hideyoshi's mother, so that when Kiyomasa's father died when the boy was three years old, Hideyoshi took charge of him, and soon realized the child's military potential. They were to be comrades-in-arms for the whole of Hideyoshi's life.

For Kato Kiyomasa the Battle of Shizugatake began with the sound of a conch shell, which ordered him into the attack against Sakuma's samurai. Wielding a cross-bladed spear, Kiyomasa confronted one of Sakuma's most experienced generals.

Left: Kato Kiyomasa in single combat. In Hideyoshi's army was a young warrior called Kato Kiyomasa, who was eager to make a name for himself. During the fighting he grappled with an enemy samurai (whose name is unknown), and used a primitive form of *aikido* to turn the other man's strength against himself. During the fight they both fell off the path.

Left: Shizugatake. This view is taken from a small Buddhist graveyard near the summit of Shizugatake, looking down towards Lake Biwa. Much of the fiercest fighting of the battle took place near the water's edge.

Abandoning their spears for bare hands the two wrestled, and the agile young Kiyomasa employed some grappling techniques which turned the older man's strength against himself in a primitive form of the Japanese martial art of *aikido*. It was a combat that has often been depicted in art, and usually shows Kiyomasa and the other samurai (whose name is unknown) locked in a rather graceless struggle, very far removed from the ideals of *aikido*. The end of the combat also was a far cry from *aikido* – the two samurai fell off the edge of a cliff, and Kiyomasa cut off the older man's head! Another *wakamusha*, one year senior to Kiyomasa, who also distinguished himself

at Shizugatake was Fukushima Masanori. He attacked a prominent samurai called Haigo Gozaemon and ran him through with his spear, the point entering Haigo's armpit and penetrating to his stomach. Masanori's deeds were recognized by Hideyoshi after the battle as being particularly valuable, and he was granted a reward of ricelands worth 5,000 *koku*. Five more samurai earned great honour for themselves at the Battle of Shizugatake and, together with Kato Kiyomasa and Fukushima Masanori, became known as the *shichi hon-yari*, or the 'Seven Spears' of Shizugatake. The others were Kato Yoshiaki, Wakizaka Yasuharu, Hirano Nagayasu, Katagiri

1583
THE BATTLE OF SHIZUGATAKE

Right: Fukushima Masanori. Another of the 'Seven Spears of Shizugatake' was Fukushima Masanori. Here he is seen charging Sakuma's troops. As a means of intimidating the enemy one of his followers has tied a number of severed heads to a section of green bamboo. This is from the *Ehon Taiko-ki*.

Right: Lake Yogo from Shizugatake. We are looking along the ridge which leads down sharply from Shizugatake. It was along this ridge that the Echizen force retreated following Hideyoshi's attack. The ridge divides Lake Yogo from Lake Biwa.

master, Oda Nobunaga, in honourable suicide. The keep of Kita-no-sho was filled with loose straw and fired, and as the castle blazed around him Katsuie committed *hara-kiri*.

Poor Katsuie – personally undefeated, but destroyed by having had a battle lost on his behalf by a subordinate general who would not obey orders, and there is one other poignant postscript to this tale of a gallant loser. He had begged his wife (Nobunaga's sister of legendary beauty) to leave for her own safety, but she insisted on staying with him till death. The three girls, the daughters of Asai Nagamasa, were conveyed to a place of safety and for the second time in ten years watched one of their parents burn to death.

Shizugatake Today

Shizugatake is situated in a very scenic spot to the north of Lake Biwa, and is reached by taking the train from Maibara via Naga-hama, alighting at Kinomoto. The mountain of Shizugatake is visible from Kinomoto, and is within walking distance. There is an excellent Youth Hostel in the valley below Shizugatake, built on what is probably the site of the fiercest fighting of the pursuit. A chair lift, whose approach is adorned with the banners of the 'Seven Spears of Shizu-gatake', whisks you comfortably to the summit of Shizugatake, from which the course of the battle can easily be followed. It is a simple matter to retrace the steps of Hideyoshi's pursuit of Sakuma's samurai. There is a very fine bronze statue as a memorial.

The 'pursuit' can be continued as far as Kita-no-sho, by train. Rejoin the slow train from Kinomoto to Tsuruga and change to a main-line express for Fukui. It will be a brief visit. Fukui has swallowed Kita-no-sho whole, and whereas many old castle sites are now public parks, the site of Kita-no-sho is a small patch of ground surrounded by city buildings. Turn left out of the station, walk 100 yards until you see the motorway flyover, then turn right and follow the the flyover. You will pass the site on your right. The first thing you will notice is a fierce-looking statue of Shibata Katsuie, staring at the traffic. There is a shrine behind him, where one may make an offering to his memory. He deserves it.

1583
THE BATTLE OF SHIZUGATAKE

Katsumoto and Kasuya Takenori. Another young warrior, Ishikawa Heisuke, earned equal fame with them, but was killed in action.

There followed a bloody pursuit, Sakuma's troops throwing weapons and armour to one side as they ran through the dense forests which cover these hills to this day. They flooded back into Echizen, and it was an astonished and dismayed Shibata Katsuie who watched the forerunners of the defeated army stagger up to the gates of Kita-no-sho. Soon they were joined by Hideyoshi, the bulk of whose army had followed his rapid vanguard from Ogaki. Shibata Katsuie knew that his position was hopeless, but he could not easily submit. Instead he resolved to follow his old

1583
THE BATTLE OF SHIZUGATAKE

Right: Statue of Shibata Katsuie. Following the defeat of Shizugatake, Shibata Katsuie withdrew to his castle of Kita-no-Sho (now Fukui), where he committed suicide. This fine modern statue of Katsuie stands on the site of Kita-no-Sho Castle, which is in the centre of Fukui City.

1600

The Battle of Sekigahara

The final battle we shall be discussing in this volume was almost the last battle to be fought by the samurai of Medieval Japan. In a sense Sekigahara is the culmination of the struggles we have so far described. There is strategy on a grand scale, with echoes of Kawanakajima. There is the use of castles and roads to control the movement of enemy troops. Several of these castles, such as Gifu and Kiyosu, have been mentioned before in similar contexts. Above all, there is the desire to control the two main roads, the Tokaido and the Nakasendo, which has featured in nearly every battle we have described so far.

The Infant Heir

As we have moved forward seventeen years from 1583 it is necessary to begin with a recap of the political situation. Toyotomi Hideyoshi, the victor of Shizugatake, had gone on to achieve absolute power, inheriting all of Nobunaga's domains, and pushing his control further than even Nobunaga had dared, conquering the islands of Shikoku and Kyushu, and receiving the submission of the *daimyo* in the far north of Japan. Between 1592 and 1598 his armies fought a war in Korea, and succeeded in crossing the Chinese border for a short period.

But in 1598 Toyotomi Hideyoshi died in the circumstances that all absolute monarchs dread. He left an infant son, Hideyori, aged five, to inherit his vast empire. It was a similar situation to 1582, when Nobunaga's untimely death had allowed Hideyoshi to arrange matters so that control passed to him, and also in common with 1582, there was no shortage of powerful *daimyo* willing to try their own hands at being a king-maker.

The strongest, and richest *daimyo* in Japan was Tokugawa Ieyasu. We have met him so far as one of the defeated leaders at Okehazama, defeated again, almost decisively, at Mikata-ga-Hara, and a sharer in victory with Nobunaga at Anegawa and Nagashino. Since Shizugatake, he had first

opposed Hideyoshi, then submitted to him as an ally, as once he had submitted to Nobunaga. When the Hojo were defeated at Odawara in 1590 he was given their provinces, and established himself at the Hojo's old castle of Edo, which is now the Imperial Palace in Tokyo.

He was one of the Five Regents (*Tairo*) appointed by Hideyoshi to rule during Hideyori's minority. The others were Ukita Hideie, Maeda Toshiie, Mori Terumoto and Uesugi Kagekatsu, but Ieyasu was determined that his should be the real inheritance. As a family descended from the Minamoto, the Tokugawa could revive the dormant office of shogun, which neither Nobunaga or Hideyoshi had been able to claim. But it was certain that he would be opposed, either in the name of Hideyori, or by others who had similar ambitions. To test how things stood between the regents and the other major *daimyo*, Ieyasu arranged a number of political marriages for his children. Political marriages had been forbidden by Hideyoshi because they tended to encourage the growth of political factions. Ieyasu married one of his sons to the daughter of Date Masamune, from the north of Japan, and another, adopted, daughter to Fukushima Masanori, who had been one of the Seven Spears of Shizuga-take.

The first *daimyo* to complain was Ishida Mitsunari. He had first attracted Hideyoshi's attention by his exquisite performance of the tea ceremony, to which Hideyoshi was much attached. He became a life-long friend of Hideyoshi and had acted as his Inspector-General of the army in Korea. He was also a prominent member of Hideyoshi's five *bugyo*, the board of senior retainers whose role had been much curtailed, if not completely nullified, by the creation of the Five Regents. His complaints about Ieyasu's conduct were taken up by the other regents who suggested that Ieyasu should resign. This he refused to do, but the argument had served its purpose.

Right: Ishida
Mitsunari. Ishida
Mitsunari, leader of
the side defeated in
the Battle of
Sekigahara, from a
contemporary
painting.

He now had a rough idea of who would
support him and who would oppose him in
matters of state, and as time went on, and
Ieyasu caused further controversy, it
became more and more clear that Ishida
Mitsunari would be an ideal person to bring
opposition to Ieyasu to a head. At all costs
Ieyasu had to avoid being accused of working against the boy, Hideyori. If Ishida
could be represented as attempting to
serve his own ends, Ieyasu's supporters
could be rallied against him.

For the first two years of the existence of
the Five Regents, Ieyasu maintained very
friendly relations with Hideyori, and went
to stay with him at Osaka Castle during the
first few months of 1600. Osaka was Hideyoshi's architectural legacy. Gone were the
wooden stockades on mountain tops that
the Takeda and Uesugi had assaulted.
Instead new castles had sprung up all over
Japan, castles built on sturdy foundations of
stone, with tall towers and many interlock-
ing walls, moats and ditches, capable of
housing and protecting tens of thousands
of samurai. Many of the older established
castle sites, such as Gifu and Inuyama, now
sported new tower keeps. But Osaka was

the most splendid of all, and was well stocked with powder and guns.

The Sekigahara Campaign
Among Ieyasu's fellow regents, the one whose territory was closest to his was Uesugi Kagekatsu, Kenshin's adopted heir. Following Hideyoshi's redistribution of fiefs the Uesugi had left Echigo, with its memories of Kawanakajima, and moved to Aizu, north of Edo. Uesugi Kagekatsu had supported Ishida against Ieyasu at the time of the complaints over the arranged marriages, and when in 1600 Kagekatsu was seen to be building a new castle Ieyasu decided that his conduct was worth investigating. Not long afterwards he began to attack Ieyasu's territory. However, Ieyasu suspected a trap, that by means of Uesugi's actions he would be drawn out of Osaka to the East, and when he began to head east on 18 June 1600 Ishida and his allies must have thought the bait had been swallowed. He proceeded very leisurely towards Edo, taking fourteen days over the journey, all the while keeping himself fully informed of the situation in the West. As he held council in Hitachi province, preparing to attack Uesugi Kagekatsu, the message came that Ishida Mitsunari had risen against him in Osaka, hoping no doubt that Uesugi would keep Ieyasu completely busy. It was not to be, for Ieyasu had planned well, and the combined forces of Date Masamune (1566–1636) and Mogami Yoshiakira (1546–1614) kept Uesugi well at bay.

Once again the issue was to be the control of the roads: the mountainous Nakasendo and the coastal Tokaido, and once again the decisive area was the 'cockpit of Japan' around present-day Nagoya, where the two roads came quite close to each other. For the battles of Anegawa and Shizugatake we noted the importance of the roads up the eastern side of Lake Biwa from the Nakasendo. At Okehazama we noted the importance of the Tokaido. In 1600 all these factors came together in the moves preliminary to the Battle of Sekigahara.

The relative positions when the campaigns opened are illustrated in the map. In those days the Tokaido and the Nakasendo joined at Kusatsu to become one road for the final distance west to Kyoto. East from Kusatsu the Nakasendo was entirely dominated by the 'Western Army', as Ishida's allies were called. Sawayama Castle, near present-day Hikone, was Ishida's personal possession, and his family lived there throughout the conflict. Ogaki Castle, just off the Nakasendo to the south, was where he chose to make his campaign headquarters. Gifu, which Hideyoshi had captured in 1564, loomed over the Nakasendo to the north from its rocky base, and Inuyama, which was on the southern shore of the River Kiso, was also a Western possession. Near to Gifu, downstream, was a minor fortress called Takehana, of which no traces remain. As Ishida was also acting officially on behalf of Hideyori, the mighty Osaka Castle was also effectively in Western hands. Finally, half-way along the Nakasendo towards Edo, a road branched off to the north, where sat Ueda Castle, whose owners, the Sanada family, were gravely to embarrass Ieyasu when he marched west.

For Ieyasu's 'Eastern Army' the whole length of the Tokaido heading west was friendly territory until one reached their most valuable possession, Nobunaga's old fortress of Kiyosu. Kiyosu was vitally important to the Tokugawa interests. It lay just off the Tokaido to the north, on a road that led up to Gifu and the Nakasendo, and the River Kiso flowed between it and the Western fortresses like a long-distance moat. Ieyasu's other valuable bases were Fushimi Castle, which was the last fortress Hideyoshi had built, and which lay just south of Kyoto, and Otsu, on the shore of Lake Biwa, from which the bridges of Seta and Uji could be threatened. Ishida's objective had been that Uesugi Kagekatsu should attack Ieyasu from the north while he advanced from the west. Ieyasu's objective was to attack Ishida's castle of Sawayama, or if that place should be abandoned, to march on and assault Osaka itself.

For the campaign to succeed, between two armies initially so far apart, each had to secure his own fortresses, and attempt to capture the others', so the Sekigahara campaign opened with a number of assaults on castles scattered around central Japan. Ieyasu's first move was to reinforce Kiyosu, for even if he failed to capture or mask the Nakasendo castles it was essential that they

1600
THE BATTLE OF SEKIGAHARA

九

1600
THE BATTLE OF
SEKIGAHARA

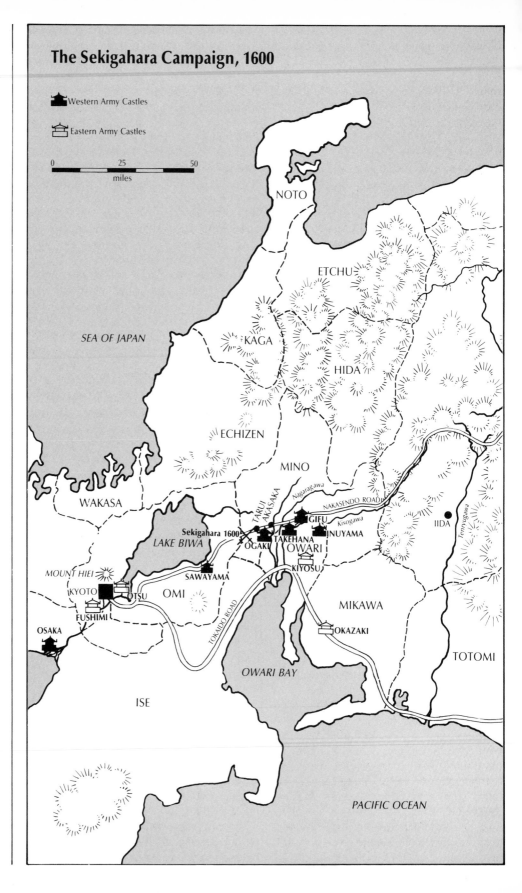

The Sekigahara Campaign, 1600

- 🏯 Western Army Castles
- 🏯 Eastern Army Castles

0   25   50
miles

SEA OF JAPAN

NOTO

ETCHU

KAGA

HIDA

ECHIZEN

MINO

Nagaragawa

NAKASENDO ROAD

TARUI
AKASAKA

GIFU

Kisogawa

IIDA

Sekigahara 1600

OGAKI   TAKEHANA

INUYAMA

LAKE BIWA

OWARI

Tennyugawa

KIYOSU

MOUNT HIEI

SAWAYAMA

KYOTO   OTSU

OMI

MIKAWA

FUSHIMI

OSAKA

TOKAIDO ROAD

OKAZAKI

TOTOMI

OWARI BAY

ISE

PACIFIC OCEAN

retain this vital fortress, so as soon as Ishida's plot was sprung he sent two flying columns along the Tokaido. The first, an army of 16,000, was commanded by Fukushima Masanori of Shizugatake fame, who owned Kiyosu as his fief and had left it in the care of a subordinate. At this time Ishida Mitsunari was at Ogaki, which was no more than twenty miles away, and had been attempting to persuade this subordinate, one Osaki Gemba, known popularly as 'Devil Gemba', to surrender it to him. 'Devil' refused, and sent a message east for help. It was this stubborn loyalty that saved the Eastern Army for Kiyosu was speedily reinforced by Fukushima, and the second army of 18,000 under Ikeda Terumasa.

With Kiyosu as a secure base, the Eastern Army could begin an attempt on the Nakasendo castles. A council of war was held and the decision was made first to attack Gifu and its 'satellite' of Takehana. Inuyama, being across the Kiso from the Nakasendo, was regarded as less of a threat. Gifu was being held on behalf of the Western Army by Oda Hidenobu, Nobunaga's grandson, and the man who as a baby had been proclaimed as Nobunaga's heir by Hideyoshi, so one might not have expected him to be in league with those who claimed to support Hideyori's interests. But he seems to have put up a stout resistance to the attack on Gifu. The two Western armies crossed the River Kiso, Fukushima concentrating on Takehana, and Ikeda on Gifu itself. Takehana soon fell, and both armies combined, but none too well apparently, because there had been an agreement that both armies should advance together, and Ikeda had got a little in front. The night before the final attack on Gifu the two commanders were prepared to fight a duel, but their colleagues persuaded them to compromise whereby Ikeda attacked the rear of Gifu, while Fukushima attacked the front, a combination that was successful. Once Gifu was seen to have fallen the garrison of Inuyama, now isolated, surrendered.

The Eastern army had therefore successfully cut the Nakasendo, and apart from the distant Ueda, had safeguarded their communications westwards by both main roads as far as Gifu. Fukushima and Ikeda pushed on cautiously along the Nakasendo towards the area of Ogaki, and stopped at Akasaka, one of the post-stations, on or about 30 September. Further reference to the map will show how cleverly Ishida had been out-flanked. Ogaki lay to their south-east, on the way to Kiyosu, so that far from controlling both roads, Ogaki now looked perilously isolated. But would Ishida abandon it for the security of Sawayama, which he feared, correctly, would be Ieyasu's main objective? To some extent events elsewhere had already decided him.

The Siege of Fushimi

While the Eastern Army had been occupied in taking Western castles, the Western Army had been similarly tackling Eastern-held ones. Fushimi was their first objective. Ieyasu had long realized that when war came Fushimi Castle would be a prime target, and before leaving for the east he had visited the keeper of Fushimi, Torii Mototada. Mototoda was a Mikawa man, and may have been of the same family as Torii Suneemon of Nagashino, though the author has been unable to substantiate this. He was certainly of the same resolute Mikawa stock, and of equal determination. Tokugawa Ieyasu had expressed his fears that Fushimi Castle would not be able to withstand the massive assault which would be brought against it, but Torii Mototada replied that the castle would fall even if its strength were multiplied ten-fold, and even suggested that Ieyasu reduce the garrison, so that the troops thus taken might be put to better use in his campaign in the east, rather than in attempting to hold on to a forlorn hope. For that was how Torii Mototada saw his role: to divert a large proportion of the Western Army while Ieyasu headed east, and took the vital castles of the Nakasendo. Fushimi was expendable if Ishida could be crushed somewhere along the Nakasendo, and as a loyal vassal Torii was prepared to die in his master's service. It is no wonder that they had an emotional parting.

The siege of Fushimi had begun on 27 August, but no impression was made on it despite ten days of fierce fighting, and the personal presence of Ishida Mitsunari himself to spur the attackers on. They managed to set fire to one of the towers using fire arrows, but a samurai managed to put it

1600
THE BATTLE OF SEKIGAHARA

out, though he was burned to death doing so. Sadly, the fall of the castle came about through treachery. One of the defenders' wife and children had been taken hostage by the Western Army, and a message was sent by arrow to the effect that they would be crucified unless he assisted in betraying the castle. This he did on 8 September by setting fire to one of the towers, and under cover of the flames an assault broke through the walls. This gave the Western Army access to the central keep, which they set on fire with fire arrows. Torii Mototada led five counter-attacks until the defenders' numbers were reduced to ten, and Torii Mototada committed suicide.

The castle of Otsu was also attacked. It was held for the Eastern Army by Kyogoku Tadatsugi, and was attacked by Tachibana Muneshige on his way to join Ishida. The attack seems to have provided a spectator sport for the people of Kyoto, who flocked, with picnic boxes, to the neighbouring hills to watch the fighting. The castle fell after two days, but on the second of these days the Battle of Sekigahara was fought, so all that was achieved was that 15,000 men were kept out of the main engagement. In fact by his successes against these castles, including some minor ones near the Tokaido where it crossed Ise province, Ishida neutralized all threats to his rear, but in so doing reduced his capacity at the front. If he had acted immediately against Kiyosu the situation might have been very different.

Ishida's day of decision was 20 October, when the news was brought to him that Tokugawa Ieyasu had arrived at the Eastern Army's base at Akasaka. It appears to have come as a great surprise to the Western Army, for all their plans had been based on Uesugi Kagekatsu keeping him fully occupied in the East. Here was the evidence that this strategy had failed. What was Ishida to do? He had Fushimi, and Otsu was likely to fall, but Ieyasu's army was now on the Nakasendo, and he was not! He was in a castle that could be completely sealed off, because if he stayed in Ogaki Ieyasu could besiege it with part of his army and move on to Sawayama. To hold Ogaki rather than Sawayama, Ishida commented, would be like holding on to an arm but losing one's head. So Ishida decided. He would leave a

small force in Ogaki, and withdraw rapidly up the road to the north to prevent Ieyasu reaching Sawayama. The place where this road met the Nakasendo would in any case be a good defensive position to meet Ieyasu in battle. It was a narrow valley where the enemy's movements could be tightly controlled, before any other roads branched off to let them deploy. It was called Sekigahara.

The Ueda Incident

Ieyasu, too, was faced with a decision. Should he engage the Western Army when a large proportion of his army had not yet arrived? A total of 38,000 men were heading for Sekigahara along the Nakasendo, under the command of his son and heir, Hidetada. It was by far the largest of the 'missing contingents' of either army, famous for being too late to take part in the great battle, and had been busily occupied laying siege to Ueda Castle in an exercise every bit as futile as Ishida's taking of Otsu. Ueda was defended by the father and son team of Sanada Masayuki (1544–1608) and Yukimura (1570–1615). Masayuki's father, Yukitaka, had been one of Takeda Shingen's Twenty-Four Generals, as had his elder brother, Nobutsuna, who was killed at Nagashino. Masayuki had no great love for the Tokugawa. He had submitted to Ieyasu following the destruction of Takeda Katsuyori, but Ieyasu had wanted to strip him of his territory to give to the Hojo, so he had rebelled. Ueda had already withstood one siege by the Tokugawa, in 1586, as a result of this incident, which probably encouraged him to think it could withstand another. His wife was the sister of Ishida Mitsunari's wife, which must have strengthened his resolve.

Yukimura was his younger son, and it is interesting that with the Sanada family we get a very rare example of a family divided by a civil war. As a result of Masayuki's submission to Ieyasu his elder son, Nobuyuki (1566–1658), had been taken as a hostage to Hamamatsu, and eventually married the daughter of Ieyasu's great captain, Honda Tadakatsu. When war came again in 1600 Masayuki instructed his son to join Ieyasu, as that was where his duty lay. For the other two members of the family, their duty lay in delaying Tokugawa Hidetada, which they

九

1600
THE BATTLE OF SEKIGAHARA

Left: Ishida's camp. Ishida Mitsunari made his headquarters on top of this hill called Sasaoyama.

九

1600
THE BATTLE OF
SEKIGAHARA

did so successfully that the siege of Ueda in 1600 is regarded as one of the three classic sieges in Japanese history when the defenders were not defeated (the others were Chihaya in 1333, and Nagashino). A huge army was kept from Sekigahara.

Sekigahara

Sekigahara 'The moor of the barrier', was one of the post-stations of the Nakasendo, which formed the main arms of the crossroads to which Ishida was withdrawing. It lay in a valley overlooked by Mount Ibuki, and the crossroads were made by a road that went off to the south through Ogaki, by which the Tokaido could be reached, and along which Ishida planned his secret night-time withdrawal. Another road headed north towards Nagahama and Lake Biwa. Interestingly, its position nowadays as a crossroads is more marked than ever, as the 'Tokaido' from Kyoto has now joined the 'Nakasendo' as far as Gifu. The Tokaido

line of Japan National Railways goes through Sekigahara, as does the specially laid track of the *Shinkansen* 'bullet train', though it does not stop there, and so does the motorway called the Meishin Expressway which is the modern equivalent of the old Tokaido Road. The modern equivalent of the Nakasendo continues on to Gifu and up the Kiso valley, following its historic route.

Ishida was faced with a ten-mile march to Sekigahara. It must have looked like a retreat to many of his army as they stumbled back in pitch darkness, with only the fires of Chosokabe's camp to guide them. Chosokabe, and some other allies, were already in position on the hills around. Kobayakawa Hideaki was stationed on Matsuoyama, across the valley from the camp site Ishida selected for himself, Sasaoyama, which gave an excellent view of the valley. Kobayakawa's would be a particularly important role. The main body

九
1600
THE BATTLE OF SEKIGAHARA

Left: Sekigahara—site of Ieyasu's command post. This modern graveyard marks the site of the spot where Tokugawa Ieyasu set up his campstool to command the battle.

Left: Model of Ueda Castle. This model of Ueda Castle is in the Ueda Castle museum, and depicts the castle as it looked when Tokugawa Hidetada, Ieyasu's son and heir, besieged it in 1600. This action made him miss the Battle of Sekigahara, and could have proved decisive, had it not been for the defection of Kobayakawa.

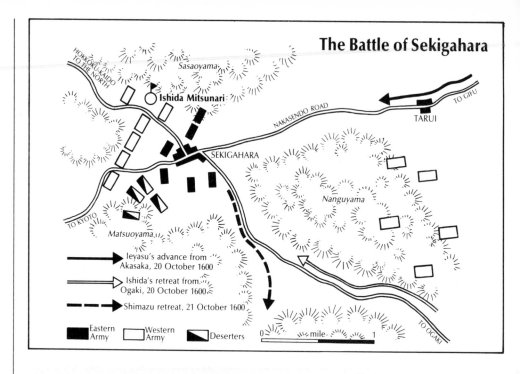

九

1600
THE BATTLE OF SEKIGAHARA

The Battle of Sekigahara

Ishida Mitsunari

TO THE NORTH
HOKKOKU-KAIDO

Sasaoyama

NAKASENDO ROAD

TO GIFU

TARUI

SEKIGAHARA

Nanguyama

TO KYOTO

Matsuoyama

Ieyasu's advance from
Akasaka, 20 October 1600

Ishida's retreat from
Ogaki, 20 October 1600

Shimazu retreat, 21 October 1600

Eastern
Army

Western
Army

Deserters

0   ½ mile   1

TO OGAKI

Right: Matsuoyama. Matsuoyama is the second of the three 'ranges' visible from Sasaoyama. It was from Matsuoyama that Kobayakawa Hideaki delivered his treacherous attack against the Western Army. The photograph is taken from Ishida's camp where a banner bearing the Ishida *mon* flies proudly.

would hold the Tokugawa in the centre, then Kobayakawa would fall on them from the left, while others would attack them in the rear. Kobayakawa's signal to move would be a signal-fire lit on Sasaoyama.

Kobayakawa was also important to the Eastern Army, for Ieyasu was counting on their taking his side when the battle began. Apparently Kobayakawa was supporting Ishida under duress, and had wanted to join Torii's defence of Fushimi, but now he was firmly within the Western Army, and holding a crucial position for them.

Early in the morning of 21 October 1600 the Western Army was fully in position around Sekigahara, as illustrated by the map on page 116. In the centre, sitting on the Hokkoku-kaido, were the divisions under Ukita Hideie and Konishi Yukinaga. To the left of them on Sasaoyama, from where a good view obtained of the whole area, was Ishida himself, together with the

Shimazu clan soldiers. On the right wing, straddling the Nakasendo, were various contingents including Otani, Kinoshita and Toda, and further to their right were Kuchigi, Wakizaka and others. On the extreme right wing, on Matsuoyama, was Kobayakawa Hideaki. Several divisions were left behind along the road from Ogaki to provide the rear attack from the reverse side of Nanguyama.

By daybreak the Eastern Army had advanced along the Nakasendo to meet them on as wide a front as the narrow valley would allow. There was a thick fog which persisted until about 8 a.m., when the fighting started. The central divisions were the first to engage, the first shots of the battle probably being fired by Ukita's troops at those of Ii Naomasa of the Eastern Army. Ukita was successful in driving the Easterners back, but they rallied and the fight swayed one way and then the other. All the main divisions were now engaged, and Ishida thought the moment opportune to light the signal-fire that would bring Kobayakawa down from Matsuoyama. But Kobayakawa did not move a man, for one side or the other, so that Ieyasu became concerned that the reports he had heard were not correct, and sent some men to fire on his division to see what the reaction would be. This did the trick. Kobayakawa sent his army down Matsuoyama to assault the flank of Otani, whose contingent was the nearest of the Westerners. Otani had obviously been expecting something like this, for his men turned calmly and re-pulsed the treacherous attack, but with considerable loss. Ieyasu then ordered a general attack along the line, and further contingents of the Western Army, Kuchigi and Wakizaka, showed their true colours. Soon the Otani were being attacked from three sides. Otani Yoshitsugu, who was a leper, and crippled through the disease, leaned out of his palanquin in which he was forced to be carried and asked a retainer to put an end to him.

As the cries of 'Treachery' spread through the army, the Westerners began to break up. Only the army of the Shimazu clan, from distant Kyushu island, were left intact, and soon most of their men were killed, including Toyohisa, brother of the com-mander Shimazu Yoshihiro. Putting himself

1600

THE BATTLE OF SEKIGAHARA

九

1600
THE BATTLE OF
SEKIGAHARA

Right: Charge by
Tokugawa troops.
In this section of the
Sekigahara screen a
detachment of
samurai, led by
Yamauchi Kazutoyo,
move into the
attack.

at the head of eighty survivors, this 66-year-old veteran, who had fought in the Korean War, succeeded in cutting his way clean through the Eastern Army and back down the road towards Ogaki. Unfortunately this route took them south-west of Mount Nangu where Ishida's reserve troops were stationed. Some had already decided to join Ieyasu, others were wavering, unsure what to make of the noise they could hear and the garbled reports they were receiving. The mad dash of the Shimazu made their minds up. The battle was already lost, so the very contingents that might have been able to reverse Ishida's defeat turned and marched away from Sekigahara. What a contrast to Kawanakajima, where defeat was turned into a victory for the Takeda by the good sense and loyalty of the reserve troops! But that was the essence of Sekigahara. It was essentially a contest between one very powerful clan, the Tokugawa, supported by their traditional allies of many years' standing, and a loose coalition nominally supporting the cause of Hideyori, under the overall command of a second-rate leader.

This second-rate leader, nevertheless, managed to control his heterogeneous army sufficiently well for them to hold the Easterners until about 2 p.m., when Ieyasu felt sufficiently confident to perform the head-viewing ceremony. By then Ishida had fled to the hills, where he was captured a few days later. It is also without question that the defection of Kobayakawa and the others played a vital part. Some of his army, notably Otani, were expecting treachery from him, but such matters could never be adequately allowed for.

Two days later the Eastern Army continued its interrupted journey along the Nakasendo for what had been the main objective of what had become the 'Sekigahara Campaign': the castle of Sawayama. Only 15,000 troops were used, as the garrison's morale was already broken. In recognition of his services to the cause Ieyasu allowed Kobayakawa Hideaki to lead the assault. The siege only lasted one day, and ended with the keeper, Ishida Masazumi, Mitsunari's elder brother, committing suicide as the fortress blazed around him. The site was given to Ii Naomasa, but was later abandoned in

九

1600
THE BATTLE OF SEKIGAHARA

九

1600
THE BATTLE OF SEKIGAHARA

Right: The Ii attack the Shimazu. In this section from the Sekigahara screen the Ii troops charge against the Shimazu, identified by their *mon* of a cross in a ring.

Right: The Battle of Sekigahara. In this section from a painted screen depicting the Battle of Sekigahara, which is displayed in the Sekigahara Public Museum, various units of the Eastern Army advance to the attack.

favour of Hikone, and has never been rebuilt.

Ishida Mitsunari met his end at the dry river bed in Kyoto, the traditional execution grounds. Defiant to the last, he refused some fruit he was offered on the way to be decapitated saying that it would be bad for his digestion. Konishi Yukinaga, who was to join him in death, suggested drily that as he was to have his head cut off his digestion was the last thing he need be concerned about. 'Don't you believe it,' said Mitsunari. 'You never know how things may turn out.' As a comment on Japanese history this may be regarded as a reasonable view to take.

Sekigahara Today

As may be expected of such an important event in Japanese history, the battlefield of Sekigahara is an established tourist site, easy to visit and with much to see. Take the local train on the Tokaido Line from Maibara towards Gifu and get off at Sekigahara station. A good starting-point is the Sekigahara Public Museum which has many exhibits relating to the battle. There are also several publications available, including leaflets and maps which give suggested walks round the site (which is very extensive). The Western and Eastern head mounds are quite near the station, and a walk to them beside the busy roads will remind you of Sekigahara's importance as a crossroads even today.

The best vantage-point of all is the site of Ishida's camp on Sasaoyama, from which the course of the battle can be studied at leisure. The approach to Sasaoyama, skirting the foothills where there are woods, bamboo groves and ricefields, is a fascinating journey, and the local council have added to the atmosphere by displaying reproductions of the clan banners at historic spots. Matsuoyama gives another good view, but is rather a long distance to walk. If you have time you can visit the theme park 'Sekigahara Warland' along the road to the north, where, among other delights you can have your photograph taken standing next to life-size plastic dummies of the heroes of Sekigahara. There is also a museum with some excellent armour, for those of a more serious disposition.

1600
THE BATTLE OF SEKIGAHARA

九

1600
THE BATTLE OF SEKIGAHARA

Right: The shrine of the Western Heads. In this shrine the spirits of the Western Army samurai who were killed at Sekigahara are honoured. Their heads are buried under this old tree.

Right: Sekigahara. A view of the flat plain of Sekigahara, looking towards the town from Ishida's camp. Here was seen the fiercest fighting of the huge battle.

九

1600
THE BATTLE OF
SEKIGAHARA

Bibliography

Cooper, M. *Exploring Kamakura*. Weatherhill, New York, 1979

Fujii, Jizaemon. *Sekigahara Kassen*. Sekigahara, 1963

Hayashi, Ryosho. *Okehazama no tatakai*. Rekishi to Ryo, 1983

Inoue, Toshio. *Kenshin to Shingen: Nihon Rekishi shinsho*. Tokyo, Shibundo, 1977

Kobayashi, Keiichiro. *Kawanakajima no tatakai*. Nagano, 1985

McCullough, Helen. *The Taiheiki*. Columbia University Press, 1959

Mitsueda, Yasutaka. *Makara Jurozaemon, Anegawa no Funsen*. Rekishi to Ryo, 1977

Owada, Tetsuo. *Anegawa no tatakai*. Rekishi to Ryo, 1983

Sadler, A. L. *Heike Monogatari*. Transactions of the Asiatic Society of Japan, Yokohama, 1918, 1921

— *The Maker of Modern Japan, the Life of Tokugawa Ieyasu*. London, 1937

Sasama, Yoshihiko. *Buke senjin saho susei*. Tokyo, 1968

Shackley, Myra. 'Arms and the Men: 14th-century Japanese swordsmanship illustrated by skeletons from Zaimokuza'. *World Archaeology*, 1986

Spohr, Carl. *Gempei. The Civil Wars of Old Japan*. Privately printed, Chicago, 1967

Sugiyama, Hiroshi. *Hojo Soun*. Odawara, Odawara Bunko, 1976

— *Sengoku Daimyo*. Nihon no Rekishi 11, Tokyo, Chuo Koronsha, 1971

Takayanagi, Mitsutoshi. *Nagashino no tatakai*. Tokyo, Shunju Shuppan, 1963

Turnbull, S. R. *The Book of the Samurai*. Arms & Armour Press, 1982

— *Samurai Armies, 1550–1615*. Osprey, 1979

— *The Samurai – A Military History*. Osprey, 1979

— *Samurai Warriors*. Blandford Press, 1987

— *The Mongols*. Osprey, 1980

— *Warlords of Japan*. Sampson Low, 1979

Index

INDEX